ART IN ISRAEL

ART IN ISRAEL

EDITED by BENJAMIN TAMMUZ & MAX WYKES-JOYCE

PAINTING · YONA FISCHER

SCULPTURE · MIRA FRIEDMAN

ARCHITECTURE · AVIAH HASHIMSHONY

CRAFTS & DESIGN · JOHN CHENEY

CHILTON BOOK COMPANY
Philadelphia   New York   London

Published in the United States of America, 1967,
by CHILTON COMPANY
Library of Congress Catalog Card Number 67-20515

PHOTOGRAPHS: J. ZAFRIR

WITH

A. BERNHAIM; J. BRAUN; P. GROSS;

M. HAN; A. HASHIMSHONY; I. KALTER;

C. KLEIN; KEREN-KIDRON & SADEH.

PRINTED IN ISRAEL BY

PELI-P.E.C. PRINTING WORKS LTD.

INTRODUCTION
BENJAMIN TAMMUZ

ONE: INTRODUCTION by BENJAMIN TAMMUZ

The artist's studio is the place where the whole fate of Art, its spiritual content, its range, its technique is decided. This studio, however, is not an ivory tower, sealed off from the world outside. It is, on the contrary, a place of glass walls, opening on to the remotest distances of time and space. The artist in this glittering and transparent bubble is connected to these far distances by filaments of the imagination, which though invisible, are stronger by far than any mere social or personal contact.

The artist, working in what appears to be mute isolation, has other means than the obvious by which to understand and to make himself understood. There are constant discourses with, and feverish debates between himself and other persons, himself and artistic trends, himself and forms, and these not alone on the conscious level. For an artist's intuition will often direct him into ways which will receive tangible expression in his work only at some later time.

Pietro and Ambrogio Lorenzetti not only maintained in the one direction a lively contact with Byzantine painting, but by this very contact prepared in the other direction a fertile field for the subsequent genius of Fra Angelico.

The Post-Impressionists not only had close connections with the Japanese print of two hundred years before; the Cubists not only had close affinities with African and Oceanic primitive sculpture; but themselves initiated trends which dominated the arts of all of Europe and the Americas for the first half of the twentieth century. The effect of these trends on Israeli artists will be discussed in detail later.

Art historians and sociologists must examine art movements and comment on their social, political and cultural aspects. The artist, however, is required neither to expound nor interpret. His whole duty and the very essence of his achievement is to create the work of art.

This has been the concern of the writers of the present text. Modern Israeli art is presented in this volume on two different levels. The illustrations are straightforward representations of works of art. But the text is no mere by-product of the illustrations. Each chapter is a creation in its own right, produced in accordance with the same rules as attend all other artistic activities, and written by individuals who wish through their writing, to initiate and maintain conscious contact with society. To the discerning reader, the text and the illustrations will be complementary, each serving to expound and to illuminate the other.

ART IN ISRAEL is intended primarily as a meeting place between works of art and art-lovers; and between art and its critics. It has no other aims, unless it be the modest one of restoring a sense of calm and perspective to the reader, in a situation of hubbub and shouting more reminiscent of a street market than of the dignified world of art. The connoisseur has only to wipe the critical dust from his eye, to close his ears to the clamour of commercially interested parties. and to look at these illustrations and their inter-related texts, which have been set down in the most unaffected and unsophisticated manner possible.

He will then perceive the endless chain which links all human endeavour, and the continuity which safeguards that component of art which is permanent. He will also be made aware of the constant struggle to make new, the tightrope between failure and success which must be walked by the innovator.

A number of writers on Jewish art including some commentators on Israeli art have taken as one of their points of departure the Mosaic Commandment: *Thou shalt not make unto thee any graven image, or any likeness of any thing that is in heaven above, or that is in the earth beneath, or that is in the water under the earth.* This injunction is sometimes blamed for the fact that our people have been backward in the field of artistic creation:

sometimes writers point to our achievement despite that injunction. One may well question the premise itself, no matter from which point it is viewed.

Paintings in the third century synagogue at Dura Europos in Syria lead us to believe that Jews who found a way to circumvent a commandment within the sacred precincts of the synagogue were little different from other nations; and that their desire to create and their craving for beauty had already enabled them to overcome all the obstacles.*

This is borne out by later designs for the Holy Ark, and for subsequent murals in synagogues. However, it must be said that Jewish artists never received any active encouragement to pursue their work to the greater glory of God in the way, for example, that Roman Catholic artists did from their Church.

Apart from this commandment, which, as we have seen, has had less effect on Jewish art than has been supposed, there is an historical situation which has had a major influence on Jewish endeavour in the realm of the visual arts. Two thousand years of dispersal, displacement and wandering, with only the rarest of opportunities to settle and farm one tract of land for a number of generations, to establish a community, and to build in one place for a long period of time, all requisite to the development of an individual style, have manifestly and seriously altered the whole structure of Jewish art.

For although here and there we come upon illuminated scrolls and manuscripts, artist-designed Arks of the Covenant, and carvings on the wooden walls of synagogues, yet all these are closely related, sometimes so closely as to be identical with the arts of those peoples among whom the Jews were living at the time when the works were created. The only distinctive Jewish quality about such works is their literary content. Some Jewish art critics have attempted to trace an impressionist and specifically Jewish

---

* The Mosaic Law came into being at a time when Judaism was struggling fiercely against idolatry in its primitive forms. When primitive polytheism was replaced by monotheism, the Commandment lost its practical significance, though it survived and survives as religious dogma.

thread through most Jewish visual art, but this needs much more specific proof of its existence than has yet been adduced.

Each of the four sections of the book will discuss the development of its given subject from the beginning of Jewish settlement in Palestine in the 1880's to the State of Israel in the 1960's. Nevertheless, and allowing for the trifling inaccuracies of generalisation, there appear in all Israeli arts and crafts certain common factors which we shall now outline.

Palestinian Jews became a cultural entity in the thirty years between 1905 and 1935. In the earlier of these years there was a massive immigration of Russian Jews, some fleeing from the Czarist pogroms, others the disillusioned relics of the abortive revolution of that year, men deeply imbued with the twin ideals of Zionism and Socialism. In 1935, the great influx was of German Jews, after Hitler's assumption of power.

Artistic creation in Palestine from 1905 onwards, then, was marked by a pioneering fervour, which was paralleled in the day-to-day life of the pioneers. Nourished by the social values and aims with which they had arrived in Palestine, nourished equally by the first sight of a new Mediterranean landscape charged for them with emotion, and, furthermore, by the impact of a homeland replete with biblically romantic, nationalistic and religious overtones, they formed themselves into a well-organised, self-disciplined community, self-reliant, with an immense sense of solidarity which remained untouched, and was even strengthened by the harsh struggle for existence, and the constant necessity to be alert against murderous attack.

The painters, sculptors and architects of those three decades were mostly Russian, Polish and Baltic, Rumanian and Bulgarian Jews. However, the constant movement imposed on most Jewish intellectuals had forced many of these artists, before their arrival in Palestine, to study in Germany or France. On the Slav spirit of most of them, therefore, was imposed the Expressionism of Germany as well as the brilliance of French post-Impressionism.

The three spiritual influences, then, of the Slav, the Teuton and the Latin, at once stimulated and intoxicated the minds of these Jews, already passionately excited to be at last in the traditional but exotic homeland of their race. Scorched by the Mediterranean sun, scourged by malaria and similar ills, they remained elated in their missionary and pioneering zeal. The paintings, the sculpture, and the architecture engendered in these conditions speak for themselves in the illustrations.

The German immigration of 1935 to 1939 brought a diversity into what had become a relatively uniform and settled Jewish community, most of whose members had originated in Western and Northern Europe. This immigration had far-reaching effects in every branch of Palestinian life; but in that part which concerns us here, it should be pointed out that in the year 1935, for the first time, the older settlers were troubled by a feeling of having been cut off for too long from the cultural mainstream. Up to that time they had been preoccupied with founding new ways of living in isolation; and artistically, they had been limited to an expression of the romance of the new country in their lives, and to a number of serious but rather naive attempts to introduce an Oriental strain into their work.

From 1935, until the Independence of Israel in 1949, the Jewish community in Palestine was in a state of para-military siege, occasioned first by Arab attacks, then by the Second World War, and finally by underground activities. Between 1929 and 1948 when the War for Independence from the British Mandate began, there were three major outbreaks of Arab violence and a number of minor skirmishes; many Israelis volunteered for service in the Allied armies in the fight against Hitler; some then went underground to assist in the introduction of "illegal immigrants"; others fought openly against the British mandatory laws aimed at restricting Zionist settlement of Palestine.

This turmoil coincided with the period when the outside world was beginning to be aware of the interesting cultural activities going on in Palestine, and when we were becoming aware that great things were happening in art outside Israel. It was therefore all the more mortifying for us, that we were too occupied in the fight for Israel's Independence to be able to emerge and take our rightful place on the world's stage. The moment, indeed, that Israel gained her independence, there was a stampede of our people to Europe, anxious to rid themselves of the enforced cultural provincialism of thirty years.

Most of these people were youngsters, born and raised in Israel, and of a curiously mixed character, on the one hand defensively inferior as to culture, on the other, almost offensively superior in their newly-acquired independence, and in the pride of their recent military victories and deeds of heroism. The artists among them, fresh to Europe, swallowed wholesale, and tried to digest at a gulp every kind of culture — for all was new to them, the treasures of the Louvre, Picasso, Villon, Braque, the arts and crafts of six or seven hundred years. It is not surprising that they suffered cultural indigestion; and that the 1950's were, in fact, a period of ingestion and slowing down, while the present decade is a period of synthesis.

Nowhere is this more noticeable than in the self-discovery the young Israeli has made — that the new type of Hebrew, the bold conqueror, the likeable, gay, soldierly rogue has already wearied his most ardent admirers; and has himself tired of this image of himself, so that he has now become introspective, attempting to return to the old image of the Jew, a man full of complexes, even a trifle unbalanced, but rich in spiritual depth, if not so physically rugged.

Painters, sculptors, potters and architects are no longer so sure that rebellion and innovation are enough. They wish now to be the latest link in the continous chain which is all artistic creation. We stand now at the beginning of this deeper self-knowledge.

Revising his approach to his art and to his life, the Israeli artist can observe a universal struggle being carried on simultaneously at a number of different levels. While Israel is establishing strong ties with the West, art in the West is becoming increasingly confused. There, a number of crises have already been successfully endured, as one or another new idea has been explored to its fullest capacity.

In the field of painting and sculpture, for example, it is no longer seriously disputed that the artist must be more than a mere representer of the visible world. He must try to get a glimpse of something beyond, to observe what is happening at the other end of the microscope or telescope, to gear his vision to the political and scientific developments of his own time. For it is these developments which provide him with new concepts of form, and with the spiritual content which he will endeavour to express through these forms.

At the moment, there seem to be two main views of the function and purpose of art. The one, arguing from a contemporary viewpoint, regards abstract or at least non-figurative art as a sort of universal revelation, the only valid form of expression in the visual arts, and a revolutionary departure from all that has gone before in painting and sculpture.

The other view, which seems to be the more objective, is that abstraction is far from being a novelty, and that the virtues of abstraction have always been present in the visual arts — that, for example, the perspective gained by use of colours alone, blue, green and violet causing things to appear to recede, red bringing them apparently closer, and the emotions aroused by rhythmic effects — the horses and lances of Paolo Uccello's battle pictures, for instance — have been known and used by artists for many hundreds of years.

Adherents to this view very reasonably ask why all the excitement about abstraction for its own sake, which to them is no more than a transitory phase, one of the numberless by-roads of artistic expression. Certainly we must remember that, at its best, the present exploration of colouric and rhythmic effects is designed only to serve the future, the researches so made to be joined into the mainstream of artistic creation which has existed time out of mind.

If this is true, as we believe it to be, would it not then be foolish to divorce ourselves completely from what is called figurative, or more pejoratively, literary art?

In architecture, too, there have been recent crises, now for the most part surmounted. A few lone voices are still to be heard, advocating the strictest functionalism and decrying all ornament; contemptuous voices are still raised against any endeavour to give buildings regional or national character.

These decriers and contemnors blast any trace of romanticism and eulogise the international style, strong and assured, rational and utilitarian.

This much must be said about utilitarian buildings, however. There are, for example, some concert-halls in this style, perfectly planned, and serving their purpose extremely well; yet suddenly their naked shame has been realised, for the utter lack of any festivity or gaiety about them has rendered these buildings no better than barns well adapted for the listening of music. This explains the reluctance of many architects to erect buildings which are only wonders of functional efficiency. Utilitarianism is being given its proper due, and no more.

Because straightforward representation of landscape and the human form has disappeared from contemporary art, it does not follow that Man himself has disappeared from it. On the contrary, his presence has become all the more real by virtue of the symbols which have replaced the substance, by the revelations of the subconscious which have replaced figuration. But wherever one senses the power of modern art, one perceives also the dangers with which modern art has to contend. So far the struggle has been silent, but it is growing in intensity.

In his anxiety to cut clean of the past and all its relics, the artist has also, in his creation cut clean from the conscious, the rational and the direct. He is now cocooned in a shell of intuition, producing objects which he claims to be inspired and visionary. The balance which should be maintained between the conscious and the intuitive, between the rational and the irrational, between the seen and the visionary, has been completely upset. The intuitive, the irrational, the visionary cannot be penalised nor called to account. It cannot even be asked to explain itself. The whole realm of art has thus been exposed to the onrush of a motley and undisciplined horde, prolific in deeds and even more prolific in words, from which it has benefitted not at all.

No less great is the danger which faces art criticism. The haughty self-assurance which accompanies uninhibited intuition often perplexes the art-loving public, and not least among them the art critics, who are, after all, only human beings like the rest of us. If the artist is by the nature of his

12

work released *a priori* from any involvement, and if his work lacks all familiar and conventional values, no matter how accurate or inaccurate such values may be as yardsticks, then the critic no longer has any basis on which to form a judgement.

We are in effect living in a period when the visual arts, though technically rooted in the past, are essentially a continuous present, lacking a past to which their present activities and productions may be compared. Equally, present-day critics are inhibited by the grave errors of their earlier counterparts, whose judgements were found to be wrong, while those of the very artists they criticised have been found to be right. So important to our generation of critics have been the mistakes of the past, that they may well submerge the most sincere attempt to criticise the contemporary artistic act. In our age, more than at any time before, the artists have had it all their own way.

Present day art dealing, conducted by the same rules as share-broking, has grown to an unprecedented volume. This state of affairs directly helps those painters whose work is so bought and sold, and indirectly all others. Though we are not in this book primarily concerned with dealing, we can show how this manner of buying and selling pictures is affecting the artist in his own studio. Throughout the entire history of art, until the present, the hasty sketch has never been considered other than what it was, a form of artist's shorthand.

Now, however, the dealers, quick to sense a bargain, have begun to rummage in the artist's wastepaper basket; and selling what they find there at a handsome profit, dig ever deeper, with disastrous results to the young artist. For many, becoming impatient of working upon a masterpiece, when they can make a good living selling their notes to dealers, yield to the tempting offers and produce nothing but sketches. This danger is added to, of course, by the imbalance of which I have written earlier, so that now, in far too many cases, we find a profusion of pretty sketches, instead of a small crop of finished works. The inner struggle by which a master-work is created has frequently been replaced by a busy and almost conspiratorial manufacture of trifles.

The affluence so welcometd in he West at the end of World War II has now reached Israel and with it the defilement of a large part of the hitherto untainted realm of art.

Since 1954 in Israel the controversy between the abstract and the figurative groups seems to have died down. This may well be simply a matter of age, the abstract group believing that their opponents have grown senile, while the figurative painters feel sure that the youngsters will come to their senses as they grow older, and return, as it were, to the fold.

Whether this is so or not, the struggle in Israel is now being carried on in the proper place — the artist's studio. That there are practically no art critics of distinction in Israel has served to calm the situation still further. This calm does not, however, imply that Israeli art is in the doldrums. Many exhibitions are being mounted, and many studios, workshops and galleries being built amid the feverish construction going on in Israel at the moment. Action comes first: theory lags behind. This is a natural feature, and only to be expected in a country where urgent practical solutions to its many problems must be found, before time can be spent propounding theories and subjecting them to analysis.

We cannot conclude without a few lines on the public, which buys pictures, sculpture and ceramics; and commissions architects to build country villas and urban apartments. The waves of plenty which have flooded the West have rippled to Israel too. People here wish to improve their living conditions, to adorn their houses with beautiful objects, to add to their comfort and to their culture at one and the same time. This is particularly understandable among Jews. Even in the darkest periods of their history, illiteracy has been rare. Indeed, the less secure were their persons and their livelihoods, the greater their recourse to the holy writings of Israel for comfort and inspiration. The attachment of the Jew to his books is proverbial.

In Israel, paintings, ceramics, and, to a lesser extent sculpture, are common in practically every household from the lower middle class upwards. Taking into account that our term 'lower middle class' includes all industrial workers and a large proportion of agricultural workers, organised in *kibbutzim* and co-operative settlements, there are only two kinds of Israeli home from which works of art are absent. They are those of the Jewish immigrants from Moslem countries who soon join the ranks of the art lovers, and those of the Arab minority.

To be fair to the Arabs of Israel, it should be pointed out that anyone who observes tradition embellishes his home with a host of folk objects, from which the Israeli artist still derives a great deal of his inspiration.

For all that, this rosy picture should not cause us too much happiness, however gratifying it may be to the Israeli politician or statesman. The growing demand for a great mass of shallow 'culture' largely determines the quality of contemporary works of art. Few artists can completely withstand the temptation of a market geared to the shoddy and up-to-the-minute. This, however, is by no means a peculiarly Israeli phenomenon, and is therefore outside the scope of our discussion, sparing us indulgence in undemocratic thoughts.

In a world which speaks with growing self-consciousness of international art and an international style, there are still many who insist on reviving the important question whether or not there is a specifically Israeli art. We believe that this book goes some way towards answering this question, although in no chapter will it be directly raised. Each chapter will, however, attempt to feel the pulse of, and to translate into words what is taking place in the innermost recesses of the living body of art in Israel.

PAINTING
YONA FISCHER

TWO: PAINTING by YONA FISCHER

The founding in 1906 of the Bezalel Art School in Jerusalem is usually regarded as the beginning of Israeli painting. Boris Schatz and the group of teachers around him were in effect a phenomenon almost unparalleled in the history of art, since they were European painters far removed from the current artistic practice of the countries of their birth. Schatz, Lilien and Budko, already ageing when they left Europe were prominent among the exponents of Academicism at a time when Expressionism was beginning to flourish in Europe. These first Israeli painters believed that even a new art form must rest on firm academic foundations. However, despite a long period of artistic activity in Israel, during which time they were well aware of what was happening in their native lands, and even in Paris (Boris Schatz attacked Cubism in no uncertain terms), they still failed to understand that a form of art which would encompass new subjects required more adequate artistic means than they possessed.

Lilien, the Modernist of the group, drew and painted decorative compositions closely akin to the *Jugendstil* of the nineties. Abel Pan tried to introduce a distinctive oriental atmosphere into his biblical pictures, shifting

"BEZALEL"

SCHATZ, LILIEN, BUDKO, ABEL PAN

17

from a dark to a light palette, and exchanging oils for paste, a move much disapproved of by his Bezalel colleagues. His was the exoticism of the late Romantic, suggestive of the work of a French romantic such as Fromentin. Based on literary notions, this exoticism appeared in new guises in the work of subsequent Israeli painters and sculptors who sought to create a local *genre* out of the distortions and confusions of ancient Middle Eastern art.

HIRSCHENBERG This academic and pseudo-academic approach, characteristic of early Israeli painting, was doomed to failure from the outset. Jerusalem before 1914 could inspire little other than biblical mythology and Jewish heroics, which paled before the spiritual reality of life in the Promised Land.

Hirschenberg's vast ambitious canvases are scarcely to be distinguished from Viennese historical painting of the nineteenth century. This was a world of past memories, haunted for centuries by dreamy sentimental spirits, and completely divorced from the concepts of light, colour and form which preoccupied the great European painters from Constable onwards.

That the first students of the Bezalel school preferred not to imitate their teachers would then, seem wholly natural. The young Israeli painters of the 1920's were without a European tradition; and the long and ancient tradition of historical Judaism began to give way before their immediate experience of working in Israel. Their aims were more modest, but their attainments of more promise, than those of their teachers. It was not so much that the younger painters wished to sever all links with the past; it was rather that they now had a future to which to look forward.

Before he came to Israel, Reuven Rubin had drunk deeply of Paris. Gutman, Paldi, Shemi and Ziona Tajer all realised that Fauvism and Western European painting from Cezanne onwards was permeated with a distinctive Mediterranean atmosphere. Form was treated as a generalization of, or abstraction from, objects set in a landscape; while colour was used to re-enforce the rich atmosphere and graphic dramatic content of a picture, as opposed to the literary drama of the early paintings of the Bezalel School.

The painters of the Twenties who formed themselves into a distinct group may well be termed the *Idealists*. The *école de Paris,* it is true, had a marked

18

influence on most Israeli artists from 1920 onwards. The Idealists, however, sought specifically to express the Israeli landscape, searching for colours and tones typical of the country, and merging figures with primarily exotic and narrative overtones into these landscapes.

The exhibitions mounted at David's Citadel in Jerusalem from 1923 onwards clearly show how far the aims of the Bezalel teachers and their students had already diverged.

LEVI-OPEL
AHARON LEVI

The names of Levi-Opel and Aharon Halevi were no doubt forgotten in the emergence of later Israeli styles. Yet these two founded a whole school of painting destined to leave a decisive influence upon Israeli landscape painting, which has been the main preoccupation of Israeli painting until recently. The work of Reuven Rubin and Nahum Gutman is characteristic of this school. Both endowed it with distinctive personal qualities which they developed in different ways.

RUBIN

Rubin idealised the landscape in much the same way as a whole group of writers and poets newly come to the land of Israel. His work may be regarded as a conclusive manifestation of the emotions evoked in this new spiritual climate, so different from the one in which he had grown up. He was familiar with French painting, having lived in Paris, yet he was not attracted by any of the modern movements.

His naivety has been compared to that of the Douanier Rousseau, but this is incorrect, for his naivety was not of Rousseau's kind, but more like that of Chagall, though on completely different spiritual and emotional planes. Like Chagall, Rubin observed subjects for his pictures springing up all around him; and like Chagall, sensed the poetry inherent in the juxtaposition of dissimilar and unrelated objects, seen from unlikely angles. His portrait of the sculptor Melnikov against a background of houses, and his Jaffa landscapes seen through an open window, point to the expressive qualities of Rubin's early work in Israel. His style, romantic yet extremely simple, is characterised by its complete adaptation to a new visual world.

GUTMAN

The distinctive features of Nahum Gutman's painting are a very wide palette used to portray local themes figuratively. Rubin depicts a bright, colourful world, if less bright than that of the Expressionists. Gutman, on the other hand, came to think of detail as decoration. His light airy figures provide colour contrasts as they flit across the local landscape. Considering his subjects visual symbols far more theatrical than those of Rubin, Gutman achieved in his work a sublimation of the commonplace.

In retrospect, we can summarise the problems which preoccupied our artists in the early Twenties. There can be no doubt that the decade following the First World War was crucial in the development of painting in Israel.

Rubin, Gutman and their colleagues took the path of synthesis without intending to do so. Indeed, at their exhibitions in Jerusalem and later in Tel Aviv, they expressly stated that the artist's duty was to convey all that was unique in the emergent life of the country. Anything recalling European art and its aesthetic traditions. and anything suggestive of extreme modern trends would be interpreted for many years to come as an evasion of the collective task of Israeli artists.

However, no matter how hard he tried, the Israeli artist could neither discard entirely the influence of his land of origin, nor entirely disregard the creative ambiences of the West and the Near East. For many years, in fact, Jewish Expressionism was to remain common to all young Israeli artists. Each of them in truth, discarded the provincial atmosphere in which he had grown up for another provincialism equally restrictive and spiritually desolate. These naive idealists believed implicitly in the perfection of their lives and outlooks, and searched constantly for that element in the local landscape which would best express this belief in the most direct visual terms.

Rubin, Gutman, Ziona Tajer and Paldi form the first school of Israeli painting. Rubin and Gutman perfected their styles in the early Twenties, and their work has undergone no marked change since then.

**ZIONA TAJER
ISRAEL PALDI**

Ziona Tajer, who unlike most of her contemporaries was born in Israel, also belonged to the group which had leanings toward the *école de Paris* (not to be confused with the Paris Jewish school of painting which we shall discuss later). Her excellent portraits of this time combine Fauve and post-Cubist characteristics, with an aggressive and quite original expressionism.

Paldi, who came here in 1909, brought with him an Expressionism more

20

nearly akin to its European origin. His landscapes with their sharply contrasting colours mark the first attempt of an Israeli painter to treat a picture as essentially an arrangement of forms.

These four, then, as opposed to most of their coevals, represent the international trend. Their work assumes a special significance in the light of recent developments in Israeli painting; but it must be said that while Rubin and Gutman to a certain extent toed the line drawn by the Jewish intelligentsia of the 1920's, and soon overworked a limited range of subjects, Ziona Tajer and Israel Paldi refrained from actively adopting any line at all, other than a personal one.

The second school is typified by two marked characteristics—the Expressionism of the country of origin of the various artists and the dramatic Paris — Jewish trend which was developed by both direct and indirect contact with Jews working in Paris, whose constant contact with French painting had freed them from the academic and local influences under which they had previously worked.

As has already been noted, the members of the first Israeli school soon exchanged their sombre palette for a brighter one; the second Israeli school under this Paris-Jewish influence retained the sombre palette, and used Parisian techniques to create a dramatic visual world new to Israeli painting. Later, however, most members of the second school widened their scope to encompass international modes.

The personality of Menahem Shemi was by far the most colourful of this SHEMI group, and his development typifies the currents which mark Israeli painting from 1920 until his death in 1951. The exact opposite of a mandarin, Shemi never regarded the formulae so hard-worked by some of his contemporaries as a substitute for creative art. Nor did he seek a formula of his own. A decided Expressionist, but with a rare degree of inner tension and bold vigour which he constantly tried to tame, he strove to establish a rapport between the landscape of Israel and his canvas, as it were to create a searching dialogue between the object and its representation, which was to be a combination of opposites, at the some time stammering and voluble, dramatic and placid, free-flowing and restrained.

Shemi's long and fruitful activity is significant in the achievement of Israeli painting. His Tiberias (1922) and Acre (1936) periods produced basically descriptive pictures, less personalised than those of Rubin and Gutman, yet nevertheless interesting for their decorative duality, in the bold trenchant manner characteristic of his later work.

Then came the Carmel period (1940), the dark colourful compositions showing the influence of Soutine, whom he had met in Paris. Finally, in his Safed and Mount Atzmon landscapes, he reverted to bright, richly-coloured compositions, broken down into intricate detail, but abstracted from, rather than in any direct visual relationship with, nature.

MOKADY Mokady selected his subject and evolved his distinctive style in a very short period of time, manifesting the greatest virtuosity. In the early Thirties, he could with justice have been considered a Parisian painter taking a keen interest in everything that was happening in the French capital.

His portraits are forceful, in which, by a dual schematization of colour and form, he succeeds in imparting a sense of alertness to his subjects. Yet for a long time he confined himself to hundreds of variations on a single theme. His ability to dramatise, apparently as much in his abstract compositions as in his figurative work, is essentially sensuous and impulsive; while his *oeuvre* may be summarised in three words — *mastery and self-confidence*.

LITVINOVSKY, ATAR GLIKSBERG FRAENKEL CASTEL Other aspects of Paris Jewish painting are to be seen in the work of Litvinovsky, Atar, Fraenkel, Castel and Hendler. Atar, who identified himself with the art centre at Ein Hod which today bears his name, was markedly influenced by the Paris Jewish portraitists. Fraenkel and Castel strove to create a mystic personal world of man and landscape. The background against which they sought to create this legendary realm was not sufficiently defined, so that their work was subjected to contrary influences and their styles underwent frequent change. Fraenkel was at the mercy of each change of Jewish Expressionism; Castel was influenced equally by Oriental folk art and by Rouault.

Litvinovsky, more than any other Israeli painter, adhered to a plan of painting, faithfully observing rules promulgated by others, of visualisation, treatment of subject, colour, and even manner of drawing. Yet his mastery

22

of technique and subtle brushwork have gained him a reputation as a portraitist.

Hendler, who confined himself for a very long time to drawing, in his search for a brisk but all-embracing description of man and landscape, accomplished more in the field of draughtsmanship than any other Israeli artist. Despite the influences under which he worked, and the persistent repetition of identical lines and rhythms he imparted a personal style to the traditional Israeli theme of man in a landscape. He succeeded in avoiding the dangers of mannerism and retained the freshness of his penmanship by a careful discovery and portrayal of the most unusual and distinctive aspects of apparently banal subjects.

Hendler's work, even at its most uninspired, shows the constant struggle he waged against too facile an accomplishment. Nor did his search for the most economical means of expression indicate any deficiency in his powers of observation. Keen observation is manifest in each of his drawings, but reined in by his extreme sensitivity, a sensitivity fatal to a man constantly striving for perfection and never attaining it.

Hendler exerted considerable and unexpected influence on later Israeli draughtsmanship. Arie Navon, Steimatsky, and other younger artists owe much to him and to his awareness of the importance of the freely-flowing line.

In the 1930's, the artist in Israel became integrated in society, and felt his position to be stronger and more assured. One-man shows at the Museum in Tel Aviv brought local painters to the notice of wide sections of the public. The exhibition of Rubin's work in 1932 aroused as much interest among the general public as it did among the intellectuals. In the same year was first published the art review *Gazit,* under the editorship of Gavriel Talpir.

The large immigration of Jews from Germany and bordering states, following the Nazi rise to power in 1933, included many painters, already established in the countries from which they had come. Some were associated with the international movements — Steinhardt for example, had exhibited with *Die Stürmer* group in Berlin in 1912; and Aschheim, a German

23

post-Expressionist, was a pupil of the German modernist, Otto Müller. Steinhardt, Aschheim. and Miron Sima came to Palestine just at the moment when Expressionism was being outlawed by Nazi Germany as decadent.

STEINHARDT

In Israel, Yaakov Steinhardt continued his wood engraving in the German Expressionist tradition. From the time he came to live in Jerusalem until now, after the first years when he depicted scenes from Jewish life in Europe, he has specialised in Biblical themes. It would be tempting to advance the idea that although he works in a different medium, he carries on the Bezalel tradition. His artistic development in this country, however, was entirely personal, and wholly independent of, and unaffected by, his new surroundings. Like that of his German fellow artists, his work is completely subjective.

The manner in which he depicts his subjects — there is nearly always a human figure in the centre foreground — points to an ineluctable impulse to make a direct connection between the spectator and some dramatic situation. It is the broken or convoluted arabesque, the sharp contrast of black and white in the woodcut, which constitute the ABC of Expressionism. This is the language natural to Steinhardt, the specific idiom of black and white, which makes for the simplest, most direct and most purposeful expression.

Steinhardt and the other artists who arrived at this time widened considerably the scope of Israeli painting and added many new features to what had been created in the decade before their arrival. They were far from being pioneers of a new style, insofar as the tragedy of the past was more prominent in their work than dreams of the future. Many of them also could not or would not sever their links with the artistic concepts by which they had been formed. Expressionism, for example, demanded free interpretation of nature, and an emotional approach for which mastery of drawing and colour were in themselves insufficient. Among the new

ASCHEIM, SIMA, MACH, BAMBERGER

arrivals, however, were some of different artistic persuasions. Aschheim and Miron Sima, for instance, despite their training as Expressionists, chose to explore new ways. Aschheim imparted a lyricism to the land about Jerusalem; Sima sought a personal formula for his portraits by combining Expressionist techniques with a free Naturalism. These two were later to

24

form what might be termed the School of Jerusalem. Jacob Pins, Yona Mach and Ruth Bamberger, being younger, continued this tradition of stylised Expressionism.

Two artists who chose drawing as their main means of expression clearly **TICHO, KRAKAUER** demonstrate the conflict in Israeli art in the period before the second World War. This conflict is all the more illuminating since they shared a common spiritual background and operated in almost identical fields of activity. Hannah Ticho and Leopold Krakauer, both born in German-speaking countries, turned at about the same time to drawing in black and white as the best medium in which to depict the distinctive quality of the Hills of Judea.

Hannah Ticho came to Palestine at the time when Expressionism was at its most powerful. When she turned to drawing, she was subject to neo-Classical influences which may well explain the restrained sensitiveness of her work. Krakauer, an architect, and student of the German school of painters, arrived here in 1926. The quality of his work reflects this dualism, emphasising at once the solidity and formal character of the landscape, and its dramatic nature.

With all their differences, however, both show an uncommon degree of objectivity. Their landscapes are representational, and they submit them to no violence other than their individual, sensitive perceptions.

Preceded by Aryeh Lubin, who for some time followed the path of French **ARYEH LUBIN** Purism before reverting to his earlier Realism, Shalom Sebba and Mordekhai Ardon-Bronstein were among the first to break away from visual representation in Israeli painting.

Shalom Sebba came here after many years of stage designing in Europe. **SEBBA** Over twenty years his painting shows a number of distinct changes, and can conveniently be divided into separate periods; but in most of it one can observe an attempt, through skilful structure and the use of colour, to create psychological rather than visual effects — as in his *Illusion of Spatial Perspective* (1955) and *Local Colour of Objects as an Embodiment of their Sensuality* (1960).

Sebba is a New Objectivist, combining the elements of both Constructivism and post-Cubism (as a Constructivist he builds up his compositions in geometric planes; as a post-Cubist he creates dimensional illusion with these planes).

ARDON Mordekhai Ardon, a pivotal figure among the artists who immigrated from Central Europe, cannot be defined in terms of any particular school. Moreover, the evolution of his work in this country is scarcely one of style, consisting as it does of a series of phases, each possessing its individual characteristics, and united only by the transcendent spiritual values common to all. Ardon was a fierce individualist; hence the powerful influence he had upon his pupils, some of whom are among the leaders of the present day. This was an indirect influence however; and no-one has seriously attempted to continue working along the lines he suggested. Indeed, his own work is comparatively little-known.

It underwent a whole series of changes, leading him from a realistic approach to a crystallisation of form, from a combination of reality and symbol through schematic prototypes to pure abstraction. His technique in all these phases remained constant. This is perhaps indicative of the artist's struggle for perfection, which transcends his quest for representation or spiritual truth; a perfection, in effect, which bridges these two inseparable elements of Ardon's work.

Even when intellectualism is uppermost in his painting, form and colour remain within traditional bounds. His painting, too, is never "literary", no matter how calculated and elaborately planned its choice of motifs, and however masterly in technical execution. For with all this, the artist creates a self-contained world, the real content of which is embodied in the very act of creation, so that all the elements of association are bound up within the scheme of harmonious relationships.

Since the late Thirties, Ardon has concentrated on landscapes and portraits, which faithfully follow traditional lines, and which in their transposition to canvas echo the harmonies they aroused in the heart of the painter. One might say that while the Expressionists disrupted form so as to render it with colour and rhythmic abandon, Ardon retained it, while striving to add a personal quality to his portrayal of it.

26

The subject is significant in Ardon's painting only insofar as he uses it to create the atmosphere against which he builds up his theme. This theme has an idiom of its own, and one which was enriched with new phrases at the time of Independence. The change is from flat statement to suggestion. The triptych *Missa Dura* (1948–1960) epitomises this phase of his work. The theme, based on the European holocaust, combines realism and symbolism, that is to say the artist stages his drama by the simultaneous use of descriptive detail and obscure symbolic forms. In doing this, he has recourse to precedents set chiefly by his teacher, Paul Klee, but also by Surrealists such as Max Ernst. This summarises in the wider sense, the work of a painter who evolved a language of his own, which says as much by its silences as by its sounds.

There are still various artists who have not abandoned the traditional approach to reality, although among them, the paintings of Mordechai Levanon are unique. His landscapes were originally descriptive, reflecting the colourful Expressionism of Central Europe. He painted such landscapes despite the fact that he consistently used a palette reminiscent in its range of that of the French painter Marquet. From 1945, however, there was a decisive change in Levanon's work. The landscape is reconstructed on more formal lines, and painted in a style which may be defined as rather free Cubism. His treatment of landscape is untrammelled, however, by the structural theories of Cubism, less because he recoils from conforming to set principles than because of his emotional involvement with Expressionism.

Since the change, Levanon's work has been a series of elaborate and complex essays repeated over and over again. They point to an attempt to create a personal landscape. As he builds up the descriptive aspect of the landscape upon the canvas he creates a personal perspective which destroys the three-dimensional illusion.

The unusual combination of the monumental and the mystic which characterises Levanon's painting is an extreme example of the changes to which the treatment of landscape has been subjected by painters of the 1939–45 war generation. Other landscapists have evolved a more schematic style both of form and colour. Among these we may mention Holzmann, Kossonogi, and more recently, Avniel.

All three working in water colours, strove concisely to express local themes. Holzmann gradually reduced his colour to the point of abstraction giving his line the task of producing rhythmic form. Kossonogi used colour to create effects and to stress forms. Avniel formalises his subject to the point of abstraction.

The influence of the *école de Paris* has by no means disappeared. Established artists such as Litvinovsky and Castel essay new modes of expression, structurally suggestive of the work of Rouault. Avni's landscapes identify him completely with post-Cezannism. Giladi merges man and landscape in a truly Expressionist manner, with a stylised descriptive line and theatrical composition.

ZARITZKY The importance recently attached to Zaritzky's painting has focussed attention on the pre-abstract phases of his work. Since the early Twenties his painting has been distinguished by a sturdy post-Impressionism. Although in his early years he refrained from taking any part in the ideological and idealistic discussions then proliferating, it is now obvious that his work was of great importance in the development of Israeli art, although it is the later part which indicates a continuity unparalleled in any other of our painters.

Until 1948, the water-colour was his principal and, for long periods of time, exclusive medium. We may regard his work until 1936, with which even we in Israel are relatively unfamiliar, as prolonged preparation in the broadest sense, a sowing of seed later to bear rich fruit. He seems to approach the landscape with the greatest care, as if wishing thoroughly to familiarise himself with it. At the same time, he seems not to be seriously attempting to portray the local character of the Israeli landscape. If he has so portrayed it from time to time, it is only incidentally, and its truth to life derives more from emotion than from observation.

Painting in Jerusalem in the early Twenties, Zaritzky developed a kind of vision and interpretation of theme in sharp contrast to the figurative and expressionist tendencies of his contemporaries. His painting is entirely free from convention, both in the matter of depicting the landscape and in the

28

use of conventional colour values. Indeed, he often creates compositions that border on the abstract.

The years 1936 to 1940 were a period of intensive activity for Zaritzky, who at the beginning concentrated on two themes — the roofs of Tel Aviv with the hills of Ramat Gan on the horizon; and flowers near a window. These two themes provided the painter with a wealth of material, and above all a means of expressing an almost infinite range of emotions from the tranquil *intimisme* of Bonnard's kind to the most dramatic bursts of colour, to which he imparts a personal lyrical expressionism. More than before, his painting draws close to Nature; but the splashes of colour and tempestuous rhythms slowly become the essential elements of abstract composition. Of course, the meaning of the visual elements as objects in these works is considerably weakened, since their appearance becomes no more than a scaffolding on which new forms may be freely built.

Many more changes took place in Israeli painting after 1945, more particularly after the creation of an independent State of Israel. Ties with Europe, severed before the war, were now resumed. A large number of painters arrived, fresh to the country. Our artists, quick to adapt themselves to the postwar creative atmosphere, began to look further afield at the new international developments.

Much Israeli painting of the time was examined in this new light. Many Israelis who had, as it were, borne aloft the banner of eternal idealism began to wonder if this idealism was in itself enough to engender an art independent in content, and uncircumscribed in form. They began to believe that their prolonged isolation had been detrimental to the vitality of their work.

These heart-searchings led to essential changes in the work of many artists. The very substance of creation was called into question. Long discussions, albeit sometimes naive, gave birth to new notions. Attempts were made to re-define the concept of art in general and the function of creative art in particular.

By a few years Marcel Janco anticipated the Modernist controversy. A disciple of the Zurich Cubists and Dadaists, he was a mature painter on his arrival in Israel in 1940. Since that time he has been the only exponent in Israel of an international trend of historical importance. Janco brought the ability to add new modes of expression to those already current, as he did for instance, in his War of Independence paintings. Here he departed from conventional pictorialism, then the mode in Israel, so as to impart to his *Wounded Soldier* an almost symbolic expression. This he did by distorting the form, and reducing it to its dynamic elements by a direct, bold and essentially abstract application of colour.

However, Janco never painted abstractions for their own sake. After each abstract period he returned to figurative painting, taking as his subjects landscape and the human figure. He greatly influenced the younger generation of painters after the war, especially by making clear to them that self-expression does not have to rely on a concrete visible world.

Independently of Janco, this notion was gaining ground with an ever wider circle of painters, strangely enough many of them older people. Not since the early shows at David's Citadel had there been so great a number of artists as there was in the *New Horizons* group exhibition at Tel Aviv in 1949. Thirty painters, including Zaritzky, Janco, Castel, Giladi, Meyerovitz, Naton, Okashi, Streichman and Simon showed their work. Others joined subsequent group shows, while some dropped out, but nevertheless continued to follow the professed aims of the *New Horizons* group.

The 1949 exhibition did not show any marked predisposition towards the abstract. Most of the exhibitors showed stylised paintings indicating a change in their approach which presaged abstraction. In the meantime, most of them were content to outline a new and more formal style. Zaritzky, Streichman and Steimatsky were among the few who showed paintings which emotionally, formally and logically followed from their previous work. It is doubtful, however, if any of them influenced the development of their fellows greatly.

WECHSLER Wechsler, an Expressionist until that time, began to make decorative coloured compositions and stylised drawings. His attempt to impart a schematic form to the human figure is, in fact, a revival of earlier similar attempts by Lubin. The latter's efforts to return to a form of expression linked to the local landscape was a reversion to an archaic mannerism embodied in a whole generation of Israeli sculpture. In Wechsler's work, however, as in that of Naton and Kahana, the figuration began to disappear altogether, giving way to the abstract.

Aharon Kahana, by the use of descriptive lines painted in a limited range of KAHANA colours, and by placing his figures in a completely abstract setting, strove to make an exact definition of form. After 1950 his work shows more schematisation than that of any of his fellows, and the delineation of forms is his only subjective contribution. It is hardly surprising, therefore, that more recently Kahana has altogether eradicated figuration from his painting. Wechsler and Kahana indicate that our painters did not readily accept the idea of abstraction for its own sake. It was evident that the interpretation of any theme would henceforth be subject to certain formal rules; but it was the definition of these rules which assumed special significance. This explains the vacillation and frequent changes of direction shown in the work of even our most experienced and individual painters.

Abstract and semi-abstract currents began to manifest themselves also among painters not aligned with *New Horizons*. Castel and Bezalel Schatz, who had both passed some time in the United States of America, returned with decorative paintings the stylised forms of which indicated an attempt to create a world of half-symbols. They, however, soon exhausted the whole range of possibilities inherent in the masterly but mechanical juxtaposition of standard forms.

Litvinovsky, especially in his drawings; the Expressionist Mina Zisselman; the post-Cubist Arieli; Abramovitz (all members of the *New Horizons*) and many others made their contributions to the radical transformation which Israeli art underwent in a comparatively short time.

All that has been said about the earlier abstract painters relates to their importance in the particular period when their work was being done; but the true value of a work of art is to be measured in the size of its contribution to the spirit of its age. Seen in this way, the lyrical abstract trend met the considerable demands of its age more than any other. It is true that the exhibition of Castel's first abstracts, which preceded those of Zaritzky, Streichman and Steimatsky evoked a certain response; but after the initial surprise, his work can scarcely be said to have had any lasting influence on our painters.

Zaritzky's water-colours provided the raw material for a number of illuminating conclusions. Subsequent water colour series such as *Zikhron Yaakov* (1948) and *Yehiam* (1951), indicate an even wider range of possibilities. The artist is now emphasising more emotional aspects of the subject, untrammelled by incidental anecdote. In these water colours, Zaritzky reverses the dramatic nature of his former work. Gone are the demonstrative sweeping brush strokes which expressed pent-up emotion about to break loose. Description dwindles as the painter combines blocks of colour to further his dramatic suspense. The abstract fragments which formed improvisations in his earlier pictures now figure more prominently as components of the whole structure. Yet his kinship with nature remains as close as ever, if only because it provides the immediate origin of his work. In 1950 Zaritzky took a further decisive step towards the abstract. He discarded all remaining representation and evolved a style of the utmost simplicity based on two components. First he has ridded himself of all illusion of depth, so that the paintings now consist of patterns of broad, clearly-defined patches of colour. Secondly he expresses great emotion by creating an inner tension in these patterns, breaking their continuity with half-tones and lines. In this inner tension we once more discover the expressive power of the erstwhile landscape painter.

Zaritzky is not an Expressionist in the accepted sense. His colours play no part in the expression of his sensitivity, and certainly determine neither the content nor the form of his work. His sensitivity is of a more lyrical and introverted nature than that of the expressionist; and his work shows a delicacy of colour down to the last and finest detail.

STREICHMAN Streichman associated from the outset with *New Horizons,* is primarily a portrait painter in the style of Picasso. Like Zaritzky he creates new lyrical values through the medium of water colour. He early abandoned the definition of form by line, and confined his colour to a very small range of

32

tones. Streichman was one of the first Israeli painters to adapt the concept of formlessness; yet the components of his pictures by their colours alone clearly achieve an inner tension.

Avigdor Steimatsky's work is one of the most fascinating ventures in Israeli painting. For a long time he expressed himself through brilliance of colour but beyond the confines of established form. Occasionally, just when appearing to be about to cross the threshold of abstraction, he would revert to figuration and paint landscapes.

Steimatsky's present world of forms is typified by linear arabesques and abstract motifs, such as the triangles which occur wherever segments of different colour meet. His planes of colour betray a delicacy of feeling not far removed from that of Zaritzky. Recently he has tended to translate his motifs into abstract shapes and to build up his colours thickly.

Lyrical abstraction was the direct offshoot of a series of experiments, which considered *en masse* form a distinct school of Israeli painting. It may of course be claimed that the introverted Expressionism of Zaritzky and his fellows was no more than a branch of European Expressionism. Whether it was or not, however, it afforded young Israelis many opportunities. Claire Yaniv and the *Group of Ten,* Haijm Kiwe and Shimon Avni originally followed the example of their teachers.

Other painters in many ways similar to Castel and Bezalel Schatz followed an entirely different course. These include Zvi Meyerovitz and Yehiel Krize, who set out to create formal values based on more classic concepts of composition.

In their work the change from figuration to abstraction was more gradual and systematic than that of the lyrical abstractionists. At the beginning, their aesthetic was intended to render figurative representations in a compact pattern, the objects represented being placed according to the rules of composition which had applied to their earlier work. It is not surprising therefore that in these paintings the colours of the abstractions differed not at all from the colours of the objects from which they had been abstracted. It was only later, and after form had been defined in a more objective manner, that colours were altered to effect a better balance.

MEYEROVITZ Although as we have already suggested, Meyerovitz systematically arrived at abstraction, yet his abstracts were not presented according to any fixed rule. For a long time he retained figurative associations although his pictures were *in toto* more abstract than otherwise. Only later, when he had rejected all such associations did he begin to paint freely-constructed compositions in which colour performs the vital role of creating a dynamic feeling. His forms even at their freest, however, retain the qualities of objects seen. Like objects, they are placed against a background which gives the illusion of a third dimension — the classic notion of depth in fact pervades Meyerovitz's most abstract pictures, no matter how simple their execution.

This simplicity in his work is not merely a matter of abstract expressionism. It allows him to create a visual object in terms of colour independent of expressionist factors. This freedom may perhaps explain his palette, which has an affinity with that predominating in Paris in the early 1950's.

KRIZE Yehiel Krize reached abstraction by a gradual and systematic concentration on figuration in the light of static structural canons. Since 1950 he has produced a series of variations on the single theme of the city. Gradually he began to produce proto-forms both horizontal and vertical of greater abstraction combined at first with schematic figures and arabesques of mosques and window arches. As he dispensed with representation he reduced his palette to a bare minimum. The white and near-white which dominate his paintings emphasise the content of his abstractions. His latest paintings, almost monochrome, epitomise his researches in both form and colour.

Meyerovitz and Krize both had recourse to classical elements. There was another group who regarded form as an element in itself of picture making. Form was no longer to be expressed in terms of objects against a background or on a surface but by blocks of colour, clearly outlined, balanced, and co-ordinated. This international trend, which reached its greatest fulfilment in the work of Hans Hofmann in the United States and in that of de Stael and Poliakoff in Europe, was adapted by a number of our younger painters, not necessarily of the abstract persuasion.

GROSS, AUDRAY BERGNER, LALO, OKASHI In the paintings of Michael Gross and Audrey Bergner these blocks of

34

colour seem to grow from the landscape and are free from what might be termed "subsidiary happenings". In the work of Haggit Lalo these colour blocks assume a dynamic force, as if the colour wished to break loose from the confines of shape.

Argov is not contented with the plain colours which satisfy his fellow artists; by combining with them textures and materials, he gives his colours a new range of expression. Okashi pursues a more distinct line in the tradition with which we have already been made familiar by the Expressionist painters of Europe who preceded him.

Under the general heading of the younger generation we wish to include all those, whatever their age, who now engage in artistic creation untroubled by the problems which bedevilled the researches of former generations, often including their own teachers. This younger generation may be presented under three broad headings, each including painters who possess distinct and sometimes contrasting individual qualities. All, however, are very much aware of what is taking place in the world of art, both as it affects them as creators, and also as their various groups integrate with world movements.

The first heading is that of neo-Realism. There are still many young painters who find the main motive of their work in its subject-matter. None of them, however, continues in the Idealism or Expressionism of former generations. It would seem that the real and visible world is not enough to trigger off emotional responses. The wide range of potentialities inherent in such reality has been fully exploited in the work of Menahem Shemi, Zaritzky and others. Levanon, Holzmann, and Avniel continue to adhere to the values they adopted many years ago. Leon Engelsberg, who works in complete isolation in Jerusalem is the only contemporary who produces landscapes in the pure expressionist mode: but his emotional roots are to be found in the far-off Eastern Europe of his childhood.

Abstraction has evidently had its effect upon most of the painters still associated with realism. And there can be no doubt that it has served to enlarge their choice of colours and materials. Moreover, their contact with abstraction has had a salutary effect on their style, obliging them to transcend the narrower confines of the real world. The most characteristic examples of what may be called abstract realism may be found in the work of two painters so far apart in spirit as Louise Schatz and Yossl Bergner, although it appears in more general form in the work of some others.

LOUISE SCHATZ The water colours of Louise Schatz are characterised above all by a combination of forms within a contrapuntal framework of colour. Her principle remains the same, whether she chooses to represent objects directly or to suggest reality by the most subtle allusions. Her colour associations are intended primarily to create a sense of harmony which is essentially abstract. Her favourite formal patterns are not much different from those of Paul Klee; but this does not detract from the personality which pervades her work. Nor does she allow herself to invest her patterns with symbolic significance.

YOSSL BERGNER In the work of Yossl Bergner the subject is the centre around which a variety of styles and a number of artistic canons have revolved. For Bergner, the subject is more than a starting-point. It is the means through which he presents human beings and things in the forms in which they first capture his imagination — mysterious, grotesque and fascinating. This probably accounts for the fact that linear components played a large part in his painting until 1958.

Initially an Expressionist, about 1952 Bergner began to remove natural colours from his paintings, replacing them with a set of abstract colour values which gave his scenes of that period an almost theatrical quality. His drawings, with their convolutions, bold lines and acute angles, themselves betoken the artist's struggle for the utmost precision.

During this period Bergner's work took on a Surrealist bias, a way recently travelled by several young painters. His Kafka illustrations (Tarshish Publishing Company, 1960) are his most important work in this vein, if only because of his capacity to identify himself emotionally with a literary work so charged with suggestion. He was not long content to develop in this direction, however; and after a visit to Europe in 1959, his painting underwent a complete change. He abandoned drawing for a more dramatic means of expression. Angels and clowns begin to appear in his work, in splashes of colour, making strange contrasts full of suspense, while still containing grotesque overtones similar to earlier work.

Yossl Bergner and many like him founded their spiritual world on a concept of personality. This may explain why so many of the younger painters should have been excited by the episodic nature and the symbolism of Biblical stories as well as other narratives which abound in Jewish tradition. Ardon was considered eccentric when he veiled the drama of his ideas in symbols, yet his work proved the extent to which these symbols could evoke an immediate response, even though their intellectual meaning was obscure.

A pupil of Ardon, Naphtali Bezem still works along these lines. He employs **NAPHTALI BEZEM** different means from his master, however, for his work is wholly figurative. Nevertheless Bezem does not simplify; rather he reconstructs the real world on imaginative foundations, with figures and symbols coalescing upon the canvas. These arbitrary combinations produce a kind of surreal effect, to the rules of which the artist consciously conforms. Elegantly producing anomalous objects and figures in a mannered style, but represented with the utmost clarity, Bezem makes no attempt to give his subject hidden significance.

More than any other painter, Schmuel Boneh tried to tell a story in his **SCHMUEL BONEH** work. His treatment of the miraculous in Jewish tradition is similar to that of Chagall. His canvases are charged with strange associations, poetical and surreal, of figures, objects and symbols, all in the most vivid colours. But Boneh lacks Chagall's background of folklore.

At first he sought inspiration in other traditions — of Persian miniatures and votive objects. Later he began to stylise his figures in an archaic manner directly contrasting with Bezem's elegance. His manner of painting no doubt derives from an intuition overlain with a mass of contradiction. The naive faith at the root of Boneh's intuition perhaps accounts for his forceful iconography.

In the work of Moshe Tamir and Joseph Halevi representation of the subject becomes integrally bound up with structure. Another pupil of Ardon, Tamir began as a sort of stylised realist. In recent years however, he has **MOSHE TAMIR** concentrated on building his forms by forceful lines and sharp angles which border on the abstract. While evolving this style, he developed a technique compatible with the austere structure of his forms. The juxtaposition of these forms creates abstract masses which are then integrated into the background, and defined by textural patterns. In addition to his paintings, Tamir made a set of silkscreen prints in which he attempted to solve the same problems as those raised in his painting.

JOSEPH HALEVI In the pictures of Joseph Halevi, the themes are expressed by means of rhythmic forms, constructed by a careful application of tones. His early work identifies to a certain degree with the colourful world of Marcel Janco in a naive representation of festive figures. Later, however, his blocks of colour with their warm tones leave little scope for straightforward depiction. In contrast to his fellows, Halevi expresses himself almost exclusively by colour combinations, and little in representation of the subject.

MICHAEL GROSS The structure of Michael Gross's pictures is entirely different from that of the painters previously mentioned. His landscapes consist of simple arrangements of coloured shapes. Taking Nicholas de Stael as examplar, he creates a dramatic encounter of forms by the colouring and texture of these shapes. Presenting the emotion inherent in these shapes takes precedence over representation of landscape.

Any attempt to deal fully with the post-war generation of Israeli painters would be incomplete without at least a mention of Jean David, and with him a school of painting based on Mannerist representation. This group includes Baruch Agadati and his impressionist paintings on silk, Schlomo Vitkin, Yehuda Bacon, and Avraham Ofek. Ofek, directly influenced by Bezem's line and colour, has developed a dualism all his own between the linear outlines of his forms and a poetic subtlety of colour. His work freely combines the fantastic and the real.

Many of the new generation have developed in accordance with prevalent international concepts. It is not therefore surprising that sudden changes take place in their work, motivated as they are by a need to keep up to date at all costs. A profusion of imitators have made their appearance, relying on the gullibility of the public, which is ready to welcome with open arms any innovation, and is frequently deluded into recognising novelty even where it does not exist. The abundance of motifs supplied by Buffet, and the French neo-realists de Stael and Soulages, have with minor variations featured for years in paintings shown in Israel.

Among Israeli painters few have evolved a personal style against the background of international concepts of abstraction. Avigdor Arikha is the first of the young painters to develop a genre emanating from a world of abstract imagery. Like so many of his outstanding contemporaries, Arikha studied under Ardon at the Bezalel School. He first became known through the Israeli love of fine editions of books — his illustrations for Rilke's tale of the *Life and Death of Cornet Christopher Rilke* (Tarshish Publishing Company, 1953) being the most masterly volume of its kind to appear in Israel.

Arikha's illustrations, lithographs and many drawings indicate the greatest virtuosity. In Paris he devoted his time wholeheartedly to painting. He is aware that the world of forms is a most complex one, built up from within by dynamic brush-strokes. His colours have the double task of being substantial and mysterious.

The further he departs from visual reality the more he strives to create reality of another kind, converting forms into absolute objects. The evolution of his style no doubt preceded the more personal spiritual expression to be found in his later work. As in the case of many other painters, his figurative work draws to a close with an attempt to eliminate all structural elements from the things seen, rendering them, so to speak, clearly outlined skeletons. Hence his dynamic outlines charged with significance far beyond the mere circumscription of form.

The struggle to conquer new worlds of painting indicates that Arikha is unable to make a distinction between graphic and spiritual concepts. His combination of static clearly-defined forms and dynamic indefinite surfaces creates a rhythm which draws our attention not only to the completed painting, but also to the manner in which it came into being. It is as if the artist wished to cut us off from everyday reality, lead us back into hidden worlds and show us a primaeeval universe where from a chaos of abstraction new forms spring into being.

Unlike so many of his contemporaries, Arikha gives his colour a feeling of evanescence. It is no surprise, therefore, that he constantly stirs up associations with the actual world in his baroque nuances of light and shade.

PALDI Paldi, Kahana, Neiman and Nina Mayo form a group who departed from pure abstraction to make a school now known as the transcendent formalists. Paldi, who first became prominent just after World War One, recently began to exploit the qualities of the materials in which he works. In 1950, he began to make decorative linear bas-reliefs. Later, he abandoned all suggestion of clear images and composed coloured patterns which accompany material happenings of the simplest order. The three-dimensional quality of the materials is not used to create an illusion of depth, or perspective, but only as a means of conveying emotion — inciting some of our younger painters towards a new type of Naturalism.

Kahana and Propes also painted in this manner after earlier work of quite different kinds. Kahana continues to consider form significant even now, though he expresses its significance chiefly through his choice of materials. Propes on the other hand, chooses his materials for more aesthetic reasons. Yehuda Neiman and Nina Mayo have abandoned form altogether, and reduced their colour ranges to very narrow ones, expressing sparse moods very common in the contemporary world.

AGAM, NOVAK Many painters have pursued a course first followed by the geometric abstract painters of the Twenties and Thirties in Europe. Only two Israelis are of importance in this movement, now known as Concretism. They are Yaakov Agam and Giora Novak, both of whom now work outside the accepted conventions of painting.

Agam paints decorative compositions on corrugated and revolving surfaces, which alter their appearance as they move and also as the spectator changes his position. Novak's medium is space *tout court*. Recently he has altogether done away with the "background" to his works, and confines himself to constructing geometrical shapes — half-painting, half-sculpture.

To be sure, he continues to propound graphic values, expressing by colours the significance of geometric planes set in space.

Indications have lately been seen of a new trend in Israeli painting. It has become increasingly clear that many artists who at first worked independently of one another have qualities in common. We see the revival of a special kind of Expressionism, one which delves into the primary concrete qualities of objects and materials, a kind of naturalism, in effect.

Many young painters have returned to an emphasis of the subject. They do this to avoid a mannered kind of painting, to come closer to Man as man, to penetrate his inner life, not just to represent his externals, to register the host of experiences emotional and intellectual, spontaneous and premeditated which make up any given human being.

Paul Klee was the first to blaze this new trail which our artists have now been able to follow in full. On the strength of the psychological elements in Klee's work, our own painters felt free to fashion their personal forms of communication; for by his work, Klee established for all time the right of the individual artist to create forms and symbols freely, without being obliged to explain their meaning.

Liberated from the need for explanation, the development of most of the younger people was nevertheless in a different direction from that of Klee. They felt that a return to the world of reality was only possible through the expression of moods in a kind of formless way. This "formlessness" if so we may term the antithesis of formalism, led to a resurgence of naturalism of the kind to be found in the work of the Spanish painter Tapies. This need of a natural raw material led such painters as the Dutch Cobra group, Dubuffet and others, to explore the distinctive qualities of calligraphy.

These explorations in turn gave rise to the myth of the painter as a kind of child exercising his imagination and painting a picture giving direct expression, from the subconscious, of a primary experience.

This idea of painting as a primary experience is to be found in all kinds of painters from the most restrained to the most extreme; from the abstractionist to the analogist. Fima, for example, using symbols, Far Eastern calligrams, and abstract planes, builds up compositions which constantly shift between

FIMA

severe formalism and free expressionism. His work reveals a dualism of the static and the dynamic, colour performing the twin functions of creating an abstract pattern and a semblance of realism. Fima thus places himself at the centre of a trend which attempts to break away altogether from rational and figurative work. It is yet too early to pass judgement on this work, which at present shows a constant struggle for novelty. Recently he has been preoccupied with formlessness and improvisations of drifting colour.

There are three Israeli artists at the extreme of subjectivism — Arieh Aroch, Lea Nikel and Aviva Uri. The paintings of all three embody subconscious *motifs* which are simultaneously graphic, emotional and realistic. This reality is of a calligraphic rather than of a compositional nature.

ARIEH AROCH Arieh Aroch's work is not yet widely known. His show at the Bezalel Museum in 1955 proved him a pioneer in the realm of spontaneous creation. His painting outstandingly represents the merging of Man with the world of external symbols. The whole physical world is subordinated to the expression of emotion. His imagery seems to grow unwillingly, subject to his temperament, and showing naive criteria of accomplishment not far removed from those of a child beginning to draw. He makes his forms by dynamic linear rhythms, colouring his surfaces in contrast.

LEA NIKEL Lea Nikel, a pupil of Steimatsky, originally evolved a pattern of symbolic forms, the sensuous and spontaneous colours of which were all-important. These clearly defined forms prevented her from giving full rein to the emotive forces of her colour, with the consequence that she changed the forms, and in 1955, while living in Paris, began to concentrate her colours in closely-packed surfaces, rich in tone and texture.

AVIVA URI The emergence of a style from the expressive potentialities of calligraphy is particularly interesting in the drawings of Aviva Uri. Unlike Arieh Aroch, and under the influence of David Hendler, she began by depicting nature in semi-decorative, semi-expressionist arabesques. Like Lea Nikel, however, she finally discarded all stylised forms, although continuing to rely on nature for her themes, which she expressed by means of a markedly linear calligraphy.

42

Line, as used by Aviva Uri, has its own distinctive properties — it builds up form on the paper, and yet at the same time breaks the form into subtle allusions, varies its rhythms, now is static, now dynamic. Nature is broken down and reformed, sometimes resuming an organised pattern sometimes being a chaos of elements-in-the-making. Aviva Uri's change to abstraction has in no way altered her attitude towards Nature. Now, however, she simplifies her forms, enclosing them in emotive and subtle lines.

Other young painters like Haggit Lalo, Yigal Tumarkin and Rafi Lavee have tried to be wholly subjective, Lavee discarding as far as he could all recognisable forms. Into his painting he introduces a kind of handwriting which smacks of automatism but is, in effect, no more than his vein of expressionism.

Unlike Lavee, Tumarkin is a rationalist whose creative process is designed to establish a framework of elements which shall portray one or more sensations. But though his process of creation is rational, the end product is by no means necessarily so — his *Object on a Painting* consists of a three-dimensional sculptured element, fixed to a canvas which, as it were, constitutes the geographical location of the happening. The forms and symbols of this happening create a provocative realism, the mysterious violence of which is almost Dadaist. Tumarkin plays up the relationship between these diverse elements with great virtuosity. In spite of his subjectivism, he represents an international neo-Expressionist trend.

TUMARKIN

Among the younger personalists, three deserve special mention — Yoav Bar-El, whose reliefs show a bias towards Constructivism; Schlomo Koren, who is a kind of material naturalist, and whose work is similar in concept to that of the Spaniard Tapies; and Simeon Avni, who having been a pupil of Zaritzky, was at first a lyrical abstractionist, but has more recently been an expressive dynamist.

BAR-EL, KOREN, AVNI

The researches of young Israeli painters are, as we have observed, finding means of expression over a very wide range. In Israel, as all over the world since 1945, spiritiual and artistic concepts have evolved which originated in the work of previous generations of artists, or which are the natural outcome of aspirations deriving from new ways of living and thinking.

I. REUVEN RUBIN. THE BEGINNINGS OF TEL-AVIV, OIL, 1912, ELLA AND SAM SACHS COLLECTION, TEL-AVIV.

2. NAHUM GUTMAN. JAFFA CITRUS GROVE, OIL, 1926.

3. HAIM GLIKSBERG. SAFED SYNAGOGUE, OIL, 1960. ▶

4. MOSHE CASTEL. THE FESTIVE MEAL, OIL, 1942. TEL-AVIV MUSEUM.

5. PINHAS LITVINOVSKY. THE CHICKEN VENDOR, OIL, 1935. "BEZALEL," JERUSALEM. ▶

6. SHALOM SEBBA.
THE SHEPHERD, OIL, 195

7. AHARON GILADI. WOMEN, OIL, 1962.
"ISRAEL" GALLERY TEL-AVIV.

8. ARYEH LUBIN. SAFED, OIL, 1954.

9. ISIDOR ASCHHEIM. ORIENTAL MARKET, LITHOGRAPH, 1946.

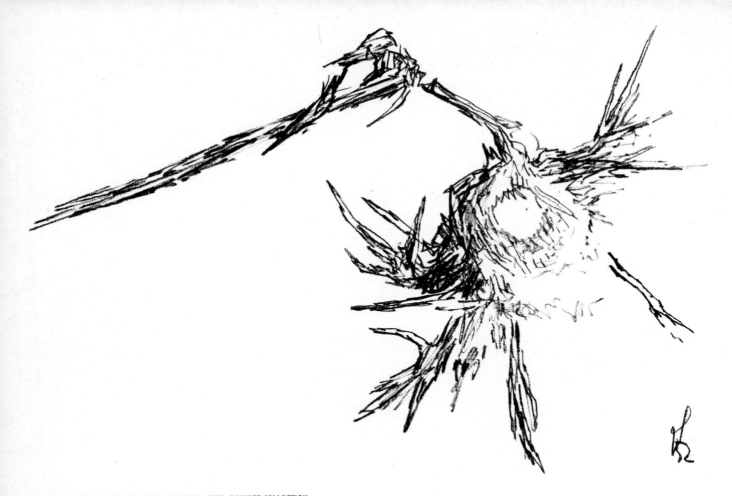

10. LEOPOLD KRAKAUER. THISTLE, CHARCOAL, 1952, PRIVATE COLLECTION.

11. LEOPOLD KRAKAUER. JUDEAN MOUNTAINS, CHARCOAL, 1952. "BEZALEL," JERUSALEM. ▶

12. HANNAH TICHO. JUDEAN LANDSCAPE, INK, 1959.

13. YITZHAK FRENEL (FRAENKEL). SAFED SYNAGOGUE, OIL, 1940. "BEZALEL," JERUSALEM. ▶

14.   MORDECAI LEVANON. SEA OF GALILLEE. WATER COLOR, 1948. MOHILEVER COLLECTION, JERUSALEM.

15.   MORDECAI LEVANON. JERUSALEM, WATER COLOR, 1948. MOHILEVER COLLECTION, JERUSALEM ▶

16. AVIGDOR STEIMATSKY. WATER COLOR, 1962. "ISRAEL" GALLERY, TEL-AVIV.

17. AVIGDOR STEIMATSKY. OIL 1959. "ISRAEL" GALLERY, TEL-AVIV. ▶

18. MORDEKHAI ARDON. JUDEAN MOUNTAINS, OIL, 1940. MICHAEL ARDON COLLECTION.

19. MORDEKHAI ARDON, IN THE NEGEV STEPPES, OIL, 1953. ▶

20.   MORDEKHAI ARDON.   SCROLLS, OIL, 1960.

21. MORDEKHAI ARDON. "MISSA DURA," TRIPTYCH.
FROM LEFT TO RIGHT: THE KNIGHT, THE NIGHT OF CRYSTAL, HOUSE NO. 5. OIL, 1958-60.

22. AHARON ALCALAY. PORTRAIT,
INK, 1962.

23. YAAKOV STEINHARDT.
JERUSALEM, WOODCUT, 1940.
"BEZALEL," JERUSALEM.

24. OSIAS HOFSTAETTER. THE ANGEL, INK, 1960.

26. OSIAS HOFSTAETTER. MEN AND ANIMALS, INK, 1962.▶

▼25. OSIAS HOFSTAETTER. THE KING, INK, 1962.

1959 יאסל ברגנר

27. YOSSL BERGNER.
    WEEPING WOMAN,
    INK, 1959.
    G. BINETH COLLECTION,
    JERUSALEM.

28. ISRAEL PALDI. PANEL, ▶
    RELIEF IN COLOR, 1960.

29.   JOSEPH ZARITZKY. TREES IN KATAMON, WATER COLOR, 1929.

30.   JOSEPH ZARITZKY. THE PAINTER'S WIFE, OIL, 1930. ELLA AND SAM SACHS COLLECTION, TEL-AVIV. ▶

32. JOSEPH ZARITZKY. YEHIAM, OIL, 1952. Y. TSAFRIR COLLECTION, TEL-AVIV.

◄31. JOSEPH ZARITZKY. YEHIAM, OIL, 1952.

33.   JOSEPH ZARITZKY. YEHIAM, OIL, 1960

34. JOSEPH ZARITZKY. AMSTERDAM, OIL, 1956. Y. TSAFRIR COLLECTION, TEL-AVIV.

35. ARIEH AROCH. BUS IN THE MOUNTAINS,
OIL, 1955. TEL-AVIV MUSEUM.

36. DAVID HENDLER. PORTRAIT,
    INK, 1959.

37. DAVID HENDLER. INK SKETCH, 1938

38. DAVID HENDLER. PORTRAIT, CHARCOAL, 1955

40. MARCEL JANCO. AUTUMN LANDSCAPE, 1959.

◀39. TSEVI MEYEROVITZ. INK SKETCH, 1961.

41.   MENAHEM SHEMI. TIBERIAS, OIL, 1926.

42. MENAHEM SHEMI. CARMEL, OIL, 1940.

43.   MENAHEM SHEMI. SAFED, OIL, 1950.

44. MENAHEM SHEMI. SAFED, OIL. 1951.

45. LEA NIKEL. OIL, 1956. "BEZALEL," JERUSALEM.

46. LEA NIKEL. OIL, 1960. Y. TSAFRIR COLLECTION, TEL-AVIV. ▶

47. DAVID LAN-BAR. OIL. 1961.

48. AUDREY BERGNER. WOMAN GATHERING STICKS, INK, 1962. ▶

49.   ARIE NAVON. DANCE OF THE REAPERS, INK, 1958.

50.   ARIE NAVON. SKETCH FOR A FILM, INK, 1958. ▶

51.   HANNAH LEVI. SAFED, INK, 1962.

52.   MICHAEL GROSS. SLAUGHTERED COCK, OIL, 1962. ▶

53. MOSHE MOKADY. WOMAN NEAR A WINDOW, OIL, 1947.

54. MOSHE MOKADY. TABLE AND PICTURE, OIL, 1949. ▶

55. MOSHE MOKADY. REVELATION, OIL, 1961.

57.   YOSSL BERGNER. LANDSCAPE, OIL, 1961. Y. TSAFRIR COLLECTION, TEL-AVIV

◀ 56.   YOSSL BERGNER. DEATH IN THE FAMILY, OIL, 1958. G. BINETH COLLECTION, JERUSALEM.

58. YOSSL BERGNER. WALLS, OIL, 1962.

59. AVIVA URI. CHARCOAL AND PASTEL, 1962. ▶

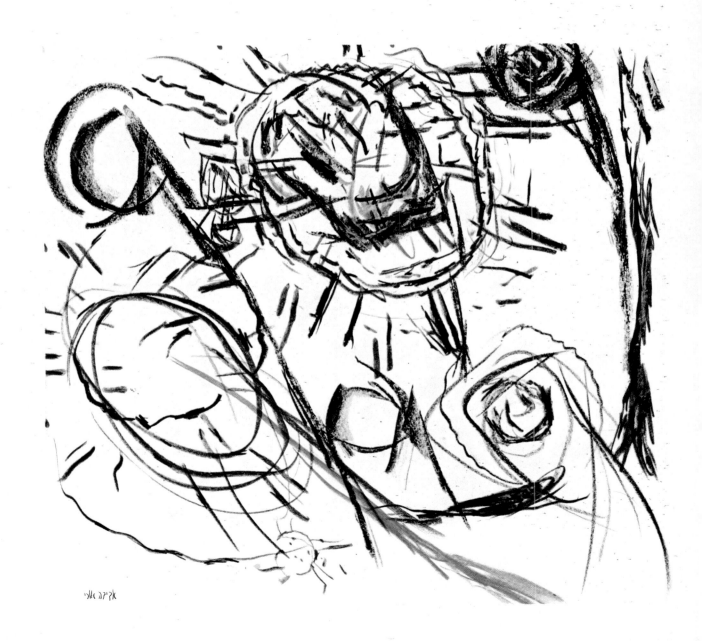

אליקה שאול

60. SCHMUEL BONEH. HOLY ARK, OIL, 1960.

61. AVIVA URI. CHARCOAL SKETCH, 1961.

62-63. NAOMI SHEMI. SKETCHES, 1937.

64.   MOSHE TAMIR. MOTHER AND CHILD, LITHOGRAPH, 1954.

65. JACOB PINS. HANGING CLOWN, WOODCUT, 1962.

66. JACOB PINS. BEGGARS' QUARREL, WOODCUT, 1953. ▶

67. YEHEZKEL STREICHMAN. PORTRAIT, OIL, 1952. TEL-AVIV MUSEUM.

68. YEHEZKEL STREICHMAN. OIL, 1961. "ISRAEL" GALLERY, TEL-AVIV.

69. YEHEZKEL STREICHMAN. OIL, 1962. "ISRAEL" GALLERY, TEL-AVIV. ▶

70. TSEVI MEYEROVITZ. PORTRAIT, OIL, 1959.

71. TSEVI MEYEROVITZ. COMPOSITION IN RED, OIL, 1962. ▶

72. SHELOMO VITKIN. INTERIOR, OIL, 1959.

73. LEON ENGELSBERG. JERUSALEM LANDSCAPE, OIL, 1961. G. BINETH COLLECTION, JERUSALEM. ▶

74. JOSEPH HALEVI. PROCESSION. OIL, 1961.

75. JOSEPH HALEVI. MYTHOLOGICAL FIGURES, INK, 1961. ▶

76. JEAN DAVID. INK SKETCH, 1960.

77.   JEAN DAVID. INK SKETCH, 1961.

78.   YOHANAN SIMON. LANDSCAPE, INK, 1962.

79.   YIGAL TUMARKIN. COLLAGE, 1961. "ISRAEL" GALLERY, TEL-AVIV. ▶

80. FIMA (A. REUTENBERG). GOUACHE, 1961. G. BINETH COLLECTION, JERUSALEM.

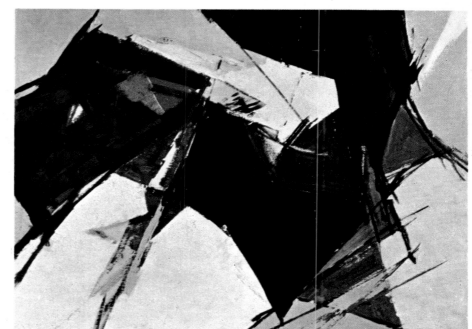

81. AUDREY BERGNER. TRIPTYCH: THE TENTS OF KEDAR, OIL, 1961.

82. LOUISE SCHATZ. WATER COLOR, 1959.

83. YEHIEL KRIZE. OIL PAINT, 1961. "ISRAEL" GALLERY, TEL-AVIV. ▶

84.   AVSHALOM OKASHI. SPACE, OIL, 1961. "ISRAEL" GALLERY, TEL-AVIV.

85.   NAPHTALI BEZEM. THE LAST SABBATH, 1962, "BEZALEL" JERUSALEM. ▶

86.   AVRAHAM OFEK. LANDSCAPE, ETCHING, 1960.

87.   ESTHER PERETZ-ARAD. SEAMSTRESSES, LITHOGRAPH, 1957. ▶

89. HAGGIT LALO. OIL, 1960.

◀ 88. DAVID MESHULLAM. GOUACHE, 1962.

90. JACOB WECHSLER. 1962. "ISRAEL" GALLERY, TEL-AVIV.

91. JACOB WECHSLER. 1962.
    "ISRAEL" GALLERY, TEL-AVIV.

92. MICHAEL ARGOV. OIL. 1962,
    "ISRAEL" GALLERY, TEL-AVIV.

93.   AHARON KAHANA. SACRIFICE OF ISAAC, OIL, 1954.

94.   YAAKOV AGAM. PAINTING IN MOTION (FROM THREE SIDES), 1959. "ISRAEL" GALLERY, TEL-AVIV. ▶

95. AVIGDOR ARIKHA. SYNCHRONIZATION, 1958-59.

96. AVIGDOR ARIKHA. LOFTY RED, OIL, 1961. ▶

98. AVIGDOR ARIKHA. INK SKETCH, 1957.

◄97. AVIGDOR ARIKHA. MUTED BLACK, OIL 1959. "BEZALEL," JERUSALEM.

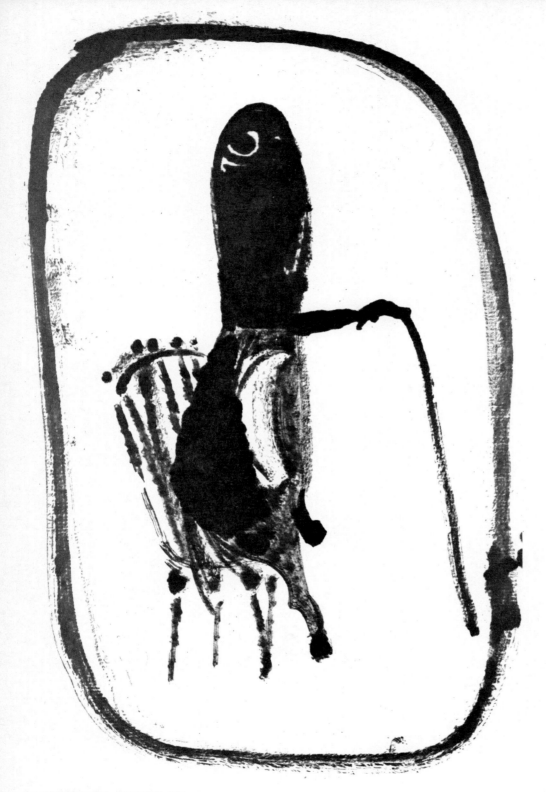

99. MARIAN MARINEL. INK SKETCH, 1954.

SCULPTURE
MIRA FRIEDMAN

THREE: — SCULPTURE by MIRA FRIEDMAN

Sculpture in Israel is directly related to the international sculpture of this century, and like it, is part of the modern sculptural renaissance. Developments in Israel over the past decade can only be understood in the light of international trends. This renaissance came about in this century after several hundreds of years of sculptural decline and degeneration in Europe unlike painting, which has consistently maintained a high level.

The decline in sculpture which began after the great flowering of the Middle Ages was the result of neglecting form for the sake of realistic representation, and of no longer paying attention to plastic values. Mass and its occupation of space, the delineation and interplay of forms, problems basic to sculpture were replaced by literalness, description and the imitation of reality. The rejuvenation of the art of sculpture began only at the turn of the present century.

The first developments of this new flowering were closely bound up with painting and its problems. In this connection, mention should be made of Rodin's perception of light and shade, and even more, of Medardo Rosso's work in the same vein; and of a number of sculptures by people who were primarily painters. This was followed by a return to Classicism. In order to find its proper way, sculpture had to return again to the quiet, reserved, deliberate, well-defined form which characterised its ancient forbears.

Soon, it began new techniques. Sculpture like painting, turned to architectonic construction. The discovery of the hitherto unappreciated sculpture of ancient civilisations, the proliferation of new movements with the new century, and personal innovations by some sculptural giants paved new ways for the young sculptor. He tried to free himself from description, to divest sculpture of its propensity for story-telling. His aim was to reveal the elements of structure and the essence of form in his work, stripping it of romantic, literary and emotional associations.

Thence it is but a short step to abstract sculpture; nevertheless, sculpture has tended to remain closer to figuration than painting. This may well be because being a slower, more restrained, calmer, and more deliberate art, sculpture is not to the same extent as painting at the mercy of changing fashion, the glamour of improvisation, or the impetuous upsurge of emotion.

However, despite this deliberateness and conservative attachment to the figurative, there are still many sculptors who wish to free themselves from it, believing that figuration beclouds and inhibits their plastic ideas.

For all that, abstract expressionism is not the great movement of modern sculptur as it is of painting, for the basic aesthetic values of an abstract sculpture are the same as those of a figurative one. The plastic problem, which played a negligible part in the past, but which is central to twentieth century sculpture, is the conquest of space and the use of space as an essential component of sculptural thought.

A piece of sculpture is basically a mass made up of a number of forms architected into a complete composition. These forms are defined by planes, some gradual and curved, others sudden and angular. The outer surfaces may be smooth or rough, polished or matt. The play of light upon these surfaces creates for us the visual sensation of the mass and the tactile sensation of texture.

While a painting is two-dimensional and separated from its surroundings by its edge or its frame, a sculpture is a three-dimensional part of its own world, and directly related to space. This relationship between the sculpture and its environment sets up tension between the existent and the non-existent, between positive and negative, between mass and void, between filled and empty. This tension is one of the fundamentals of sculptural thought.

There can be a variety of relationships between a sculpture and its environment. It can be a solid mass of stone or wood shaped from the outside; but equally it can be space enclosed by a shell, as it were, a vase or a building or their non-utilitarian but formal equivalents.

The form of a piece of sculpture may be perceived as a single thing, even though it consists of several components; but it may also be a composite structure with the individual components maintaining their individuality within the unity of the piece.

The sculptural tradition of the past was predicated on form and mass alone constituting the essence of sculpture, with tension concentrated in the contact between the outer contour of the mass and the space surrounding it, this space being passive, and providing no more than a setting for the piece. Contemporaries, however, have transformed space into an active factor in their work, by making it an integral part of their sculpture.

This is done in a number of ways and its effect therefore varies accordingly. The mass may be opened from within to form a countermass of space. Spaces may pierce the solid mass from without, and appear to consume it. The solid mass may be altogether done away with, and replaced by a kind of "drawing-in-space" with a solid material. These 'lines' of material trap space to create a three-dimensional construction. The solid mass has become defined space.

In this sculpture of defined space, the sole task of the material is to provide a skeleton, to define ghostly masses. One of the basic qualities of sculpture, tactileness, has been lost by this new method. Abstract sculpture is more appreciated for its lack of mass and solidity; so that it has become drawing in space, to be apprehended chiefly through the emotions rather than through the senses.

This new approach to space in twentieth century sculpture provides a multitude of possibilities for expression in the open, where sculpture can stand free of walls or buildings, and make positive statements, constituting a challenge to space by its very existence.

The structural foundations of an artistic creation do not determine its emotional character. Each artist finds his personal mode of expression within the structural boundaries. Today the open form replaces the mass, and linear outlines are becoming more common. Lack of solidity, sculpting with space, must lead to more impetuous, spontaneous and emotional expression, such as we already see in painting. The deliberate, quiet and steady formalism of sculpture at the turn of the century is now being replaced by an amorphous, transitory and apparently fortuitous image.

Such imagery is directly related to a swing towards the baroque which has recently been evident in both painting and sculpture. In sculpture its effect is somewhat contradictory, for the essential nature of sculpture is stable. Nevertheless, it is capable of adapting baroque expression to its own ends, as is proved by the great sculpture of the baroque period. This ties up with the breaking down of masses and the introduction of space as an active element; the active role of space in seventeenth and eighteenth century art is well-known.

Just as the Impressionists used light to demolish the material solidity of forms, so sculptors are now using free space to demolish the material, qualities of mass and volume. There are hosts of sculptures vibrating with lines and planes which are engulfed by and disappear into each other in such a way that the work is no longer isolated from circumambient space.

It is not by chance that motion has been introduced into contemporary art. Also typically baroque, motion is expressed in sculpture in a number of ways, from the Futurist illusion of movement in the work of Boccioni, through states of arrested motion — the flight of Brancusi's bird or its crystalline form in Gabo's work; through the powerful tempestuousness of the Expressionsts; to the airy passivity of motion in the work of Calder, and its machine-operated activity in the work of Tinguely and others.

Notwithstanding the sculptor's conservative use of old media — stone, wood, clay, wax, bronze — and techniques, new materials and techniques have been introduced — the extensive use of poured concrete and artificial stone, for example, constructions in iron and soldered metals, plastics, the combination of several materials in a single work, and the assemblage of discarded objects, including wood shavings and scrap metal.

The solution of all problems in sculpture is dependent upon the soundness or otherwise of the plastic values of the sculptor and his skill in proportioning and balancing them. These values determine whether a work is quiet and restrained or stormy and emotional; soft or hard; pronounced or restrained; charming and decorative or powerful and strong. Artistic expression is conveyed by the proportion and balance between the following concepts, qualities and processes:

Emotion	Thought
Sensation	Knowledge
Agitation	Deliberation
Amorphous	Formal
Temporary	Permanent
Static	Dynamic
Tension	Relaxation
Mass	Space
Volume	Void
Weight	Weightlessness
Vertical	Horizontal
Organic	Geometric
Level	Undulant
Convex	Concave
Protuberance	Depression
Light	Heavy
Illumination	Chiaroscuro
Smooth	Rough
Strength	Weakness
Coarse	Refined
Simple	Complex
Uniform	Eccentric
Two Dimensional	Three Dimensional

These general problems are reflected in the sculpture of Israel just as elsewhere.

Despite the growing tendency to disregard geographical boundaries in art, and despite the growth of an international style of sculpture, local traditions obviously contribute to the forms of art in certain countries. Israel is not one of these.

There was little sculpture in ancient Israel, because of the time-honoured religious prohibition, and that little was produced under the influence of other artistic powers of the Middle East. Israeli sculpture of ancient times is on a small scale, craftwork on ritual objects or engraving on tombstones.

When Israeli sculptors began to work at the turn of the century, then, they found themselves in the absence of a Jewish tradition, compelled to draw on foreign sources. There are, of course, numerous prominent modern sculptors who are Jews, but their work is marked by the cultures and traditions of the countries in which they were born, or where they now live and work. If there is an original Jewish element common to them all, it requires much specialist research to discover, and is extremely difficult to define.

The history of sculpture, like the history of all art in Israel, is as yet too short for there to have been created an Israeli tradition. In any event, many national boundaries have faded away in this century, and art now aspires to encompass the whole world as it becomes the expression of an era rather than a language exclusive to any one people. In these circumstances, it will be twice as hard for Israeli art to form national characteristics in the future.

International artistic concepts, which indicate the fertility and richness of contemporary art, exist in Israel as much as elsewhere, with all their contrasts and extremes. Figuration and nonfiguration; the realist and the abstract; emotional romantic expressionism and the heroic expression of social realism; restrained classicism consisting of full, serene forms and a decorative approach; the distortion of figuration for the sake of clearer expression; simple, unified, concentrated pieces and complex constructions; solid massive statements and the delimitation of space by lines and planes — all are to be found in Israeli art. All the modern methods and media are employed by our sculptors today, but for many years figurative realism dominated Israeli sculpture.

This emerged with the first experiments of Boris Schatz, founder of the Bezalel School of Arts and Crafts, who worked on Jewish themes in a romantic naturalistic manner. Aharon Melnikov fashioned the country's

142

first modern monument, the statue of a lion to commemorate the defenders of Tel-Hai. Here there was a desire to return to the sculptural manner of the ancient world; but Melnikov left Israel in 1934.

Batya Lishansky continued the impressionist tradition in her portraits and monuments. Another type of realistic expression appears in the heroic monuments full of pathos, by the creator of the Warsaw Ghetto Memorial—Nathan Rappaport.

Aryeh Merzer works in beaten copper reliefs akin to primitive folk art, in which he conveys the Diaspora's longings for the small Jewish village, and its reflections in modern Safed. The classical spirit found its expression, until recently, in the full-bodied figures of Moshe Ziffer, a kind of work which he has now, however, abandoned in his new approach to sculpture.

Another member of this school is Aharon Priver, with his decorative, softly-rounded female figures. Yaakov Luchansky made a serious contribution in the same vein when he arrived in this country, an old man it is true, but still in full possession of his creative powers. He continues to make quiet likenesses in the best classical tradition of France. Michael Kara, Kaethe Ephraim-Marcus, Yana Schacharal-Hilman and Miriam Kiffer may also be included in this group.

The first to stylise his figurative work by the distortion and exaggeration of natural forms was Ze'ev Ben Zvi, who died some ten years ago. Hava Mehutan also is engaged in a search for simplicity of form. She distorts and generalises in a daring yet reserved manner. Shoshanna Heimann is also concerned with generalisation and the concentration of forms in her wooden sculpture. Ruth Tsarfati, after searching for powerful expressive forms has now turned to a neo-baroque refined realism. Rudolf Lehmann's talents are concentrated in compact bird and animal figures. Another animal sculptor, Reznik is loyal to reality, which he clothes in an aura of tenderness and romance.

Meir Dahan who displayed much talent in pure sculpture, in representational reliefs, and in commercial art, died prematurely last year. More abstract concepts are to be found in the work of Moshe Sternschuss, who begins with a realistic basis which he develops into near-abstract masses. Eli Ilan is a young sculptor who develops his realistic bases in a more organic way.

During recent years many Israeli sculptors have abandoned the figurative approach to their work altogether. Yitzhak Danziger and Yehiel Shemi, followed by Feigin and Elul Kosso are the standard-bearers of absolute abstraction. Their work reveals the increasing predominance of the new concept of space. Their sculpture is usually linear and often made of welded iron. Danziger in particular has blazed a new trail in Israeli sculpture and influenced many of the younger generation by the versatility, dynamics and power of his calmly planned creations.

David Palombo sometimes works in welded metal, but has not neglected stone and wood, and has occasionally used other less traditional materials. Zahara Schatz, who is chiefly a commercial artist, is more extreme in the matter of materials. For her pure sculpture, always abstract, she uses plastics. Tumarkin, who belongs to a group which uses scrap-metal now devotes most of his time to three-dimensional painting. Among other abstract sculptors, mention must be made of Yaakov Leible and Robert Baser, who are geometrical abstractionists, and Aharon Ashkenazi, whose approach is more organic than geometric.

Many of our sculptors are at present associated with the abstract school. This is a comparatively recent phenomenon, most of them coming to abstraction after a sharp break with their artistic pasts, with no real period of transition, and sometimes with no apparent artistic links with that past. For many, the shift to the abstract was connected with a search for new materials, among which welded iron figures prominently, for it lends itself particularly to the solution of spatial problems.

BATYA LISHANSKY Batya Lishansky was among the first to design a memorial in this country — at Hulda. Her latest is at Kfar Yehoshua. She has remained loyal to a realist and impressionist approach, her work belonging to the 1920's in spirit and the romantic pioneering of the pre-State period. Her love of her subject, which she will not sacrifice for the sake of style or for the sake of abstraction, impels her to shape her portraits, figures and animal pieces with a light, caressing touch.

MOSHE ZIFFER Moshe Ziffer received a European education in abstraction between the two wars. Immediately after his notions of art had formed, he turned to figurative realism in the classical style. Abstractions of his early period included terra

144

cotta jugs and jug-shaped figures, and this element remained in his works when he adopted other materials, such as clay, plaster and stone. He creates full forms in closed, well-balanced compositions, and in the classic mode. His full nudes have rounded physical features and quiet transitional planes. His portraits, with harmonious proportions are true to life. All these things characterised his work until a very short time ago. Recently, however, Ziffer has attempted to evolve a technique for non-figurative and abstract sculpture. He has not given up the materials he previously used, but using them advances towards solutions of new problems. He now fashions well-defined abstracts, with bold transitions and angular and contrasting planes.

Space is the decisive factor in his work but unlike many of his colleagues who, as they devote themselves more and more to welded metal have altogether abandoned masses and ideas of volume, Ziffer does not neglect these elements, but continues to develop them to contrast with, rather than to complement, spatial forms. Nevertheless, an organic element remains in his sculpture to remind the viewer of associations with the images and forms of the familiar external world.

Aharon Priver is true to the classical figurative approach, taking as his central theme the female face and body. His portraits are marked by great quietude and repose, and have no sharp angles or bold movement. He seeks neither tension nor contrast and avoids complications. His forms are soft, round and smooth, embellished here and there with anatomical details of face or body incised in the stone. The only contrast he allows himself is one of texture, making some parts of his surface rough, others smooth. He works primarily in cast stone, and has recently been carving it directly. The more he has used stone, the more compact have become his figures. He preserves the mass of his medium without losing the rounded softness of the subject. In his diligent preservation of the mass in his sculpture he has not opened up the solidity of his pieces nor allowed space to penetrate them.

In his seventies, Yaakov Luchansky, a mature artist of the *école de Paris,* immigrated to Palestine, bringing with him the finest French values. He is one of the most prominent representatives of the classic school in Israel, remaining loyal to its traditions, in the reserved charm and rounded features

AHARON PRIVER

YAAKOV LUCHANSKY

145

of his restful figures, and the clear harmonious proportions of his sensitive pieces. His portrait busts convey both a nice feeling of volume and of the character of the sitter.

ZE'EV BEN-ZVI   The work of Ze'ev Ben-Zvi, who died ten years ago, is a cornerstone of Israeli sculpture. From the beginning, his search for form, his stylisation, and his quasi-Cubist treatment of heads, created fresh sculptural problems. He sculpted by cutting crystal-like facets to represent facial features. His forms are based on the contrast between straight lines and curves, on the division of planes, and on the play of light, in places reflected, in other places absorbed by the changing surfaces. Avoiding detail, and aided by a sense of the monumental, he executed a great many portrait busts. The essence of his technique is found at its fullest in the memorial to the children of the Diaspora in the village of Mishmar Ha'emek.

HAVA MEHUTTAN   Hava Mehuttan produces figurative forms; human figures and portrait heads in which the basic forms of the subject are preserved despite distortions and abstractions. Condensing and altering a figure for the sake of the composition and the interplay of planes, she sometimes makes constructions which are almost abstract. Equally, though, she is capable of transmitting, by means of a few combined planes or a light silhouette, the realistic suggestion of a human figure, which remains the perennial basis of her work and determines the nature of her compositions.

Her world is boldly populated with expressive persons. To achieve this expressiveness she distorts the subjects and dissociates them from external reality, while adapting them to her personal concept of the real. In her figures of wood or stone, she always preserves a sense of mass, and of the texture of the material. Occasionally she gives them a smooth polish which unites their component forms. Sometimes, and particularly in her recent work, she leaves the surface in its natural state, emphasising the rawness of the material and leaving chisel marks clearly visible. Withal she never loses the softness and flexibility of the forms and planes which create the subtlety of any given piece.

Working in clay for firing, she makes sculpture with hollow centres. She uses a potter's approach to this material and conceives of creation as a building-up of hollow vase segments. Her expressiveness in this medium

146

100. MEDARDO ROSSO. BOOKMAKER.

102. GERMAINE FICHIER. THE BAT, 1947.

103. BERTO LARDERRA. SCULPTURE, 1952.

101. HENRY MOORE. KNEELING FIGURE 1938, LONDON.

104. ANTOINE PEVSNER. MODEL FOR THE MONUMENT OF THE UNKNOWN PRISONER, 1952.

106. CONSTANTIN BRANCUSI.
BIRD, 1940.

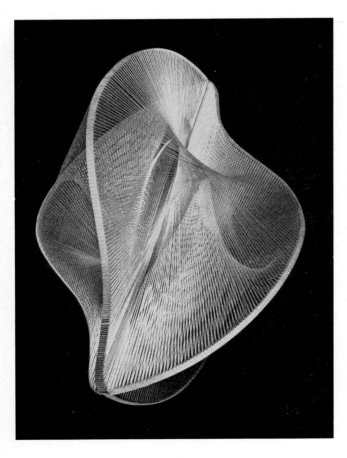

105. NAHUM GABO. LINEAR STRUCTURE IN SPACE, 1949.

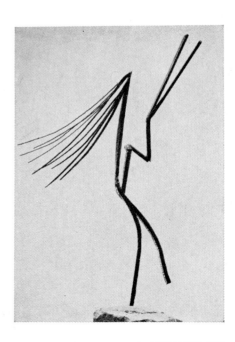

107. JULIO GONZALEZ. DANCER WITH FLYING HAIR, 1932.

results from her strict control of formal relationships and the bold dynamism they embody.

In her most recent work, she assembles her sculpture from a number of separate simple forms placed upon one another or side by side, creating strong tension with their contrasts and near-abstract simplicity. At the same time, she clings to the organic and basically figurative which always endow her creations with something of human warmth.

Her work shows no evidence whatever of the soft femininity to be observed in that of many women sculptors. It is formal and determined, revealing no hesitations, doubts, or halfway thoughts. Form and mass are clearly defined in her sculpture which possesses a solid massive earthy feeling.

Shoshanna Heimann's principle medium is wood, its natural beauty and primal form being preserved in her sculpture. She takes great pains not to lose the spirit of the material — its mass and its planes. Recently she has introduced space, but without tampering with the bulky feeling of the wood. In her very recent work, however, she has more strongly emphasised the hollows. She gives her pieces a feeling of weightlessness by mounting them in the air on single supports. They do not therefore contradict the feeling of space by the wood's solidity, but rather, the massive figures hover in the air, and therefore appear spacious. She increasingly avoids realistic detail in her figures and concentrates on basic form. Her work possesses repose, immobility and a certain serene weight. **SHOSHANNA HEIMANN**

The sculpture of Ruth Tsarfati is bold in form and accentuation. Her work, especially the figures of young children, is gradually becoming more baroque. In her wooden figurines which combine art and craft, she maintains a feeling for form by a simplicity of construction, with a decorative charm suitable to this kind of work. **RUTH TSARFATI**

Her human heads are very forceful, and constructed with sharp transitions from light to shade. Recently her sculpture has become more rounded; the forms are as clearly defined as before, but the transitions softer and more delicate. A figurative artist, Ruth Tsarfati has remained true to reality, but she understands how to distort and model it to her requirements. Her style is the direct outcome of the character of her subject, to which she attaches great importance. Her work is never a play of forms for their own sake.

Generally she is aware of mass, but she introduces space by drilling holes in the solid, or by stretching out a limb. Movement is becoming ever more important in her sculpture. Her method of design is to contrast angularity with curves; however, while angularity previously predominated, her forms have now become delicately curved.

In the search for new values, sculpture in Israel has lost one of its primary qualities, and one which in the past formed a basis for differentiating between painting and sculpture. It is that of mass and volume defined by an outer shell. As we look at the sculpture of any past culture, it is that quality which arouses an instinct in us to caress the sculpture, to run our hands over its surfaces as they merge into each other. It is a special urge to join the senses of sight and touch as though we·found our vision inadequate and wished to trace the movements of the sculptor's hands as he modelled or carved the piece.

The attempt to master space, the concern with the delineation of space, the stress on movement, and the treatment of fragmented jagged surfaces have caused this feeling of solidity, the quietude and simplicity of form, the sensuous handling which is the embodiment of the sensation of mass, to be forgotten.

RUDOLF LEHMANN Rudolf Lehmann is a sculptor who has neither rejected nor sacrificed these values. On the contrary, he concentrates on making more and more use of them, and emphasising them to the extent that it is almost impossible to see his sculpture without feeling a need to stroke and caress it.

He is now seeking the compact solidity which has always been an element in his work, in the bodies of animals and birds, abandoning the human form altogether. He is perhaps doing this in order to free himself from the shackles of expressionism which are so strongly bound up in Israel with the human figure, and in order to be able to concentrate on the pure problems of organic form as they appear in the animal world. His preferred choice is birds, the simple ellipsoid shape of which fascinates him. He finds in it a treasury of forms, angles and volumes concentrated in a closed compact mass.

Despite his being an animal sculptor, his principal interest is form rather than movement. Once in a while we find a vague suggestion of decoration in the detail of a creature's body; and even then this never mars the completeness, the unity of the form.

His favourite medium is wood; its organic warmth is well-suited to this sculptor's mode. He smoothes, polishes and caresses the form until it reaches its final state. The tension of Lehmann's closed forms may have originated in his work in ceramic and clay.

Despite the temptation inherent in his subject, his work is devoid of sweetness, and he eliminates trivial decorativeness from his miniatures by the simplicity and compactness of his forms. The classical enclosed form with gradual surface transitions embodies monumentality, solidity and permanence. His work is characterised by a great sensitiveness of feeling, and his masses exude restrained power.

Moshe Sternschuss was the first sculptor in this country to abandon (in the early Forties) realism in favour of form for form's sake He began to stylise his sculpture, to transform the torsos and limbs of his figures into geometrical forms — cylinders, spheres and cones — which he composed in a manner somewhat reminiscent of cubism. **MOSHE STERNSCHUSS**

Despite his penchant for geometrical shapes his forms are basically organic and true to their models, the bodies of men and beasts. Although a pioneer of abstract sculpture in this country, he never made non-figurative work divorced from reality. Organic forms, the bodies of man and beast, remained the starting point of his work.

His sculptures comprised a number of conjoined forms each complete in itself and with the joins not only exposed but even accentuated. He uses nearly all the materials of the sculptor's workshop — stone, clay, bronze, concrete and soldered iron.

Yitzhak Danziger is one of the key figures of Israeli art. He is a highly gifted, versatile artist, who influenced the younger generation of native sculptors. Despite the consistent traits manifest in all that he does, each new work reveals a new set of problems and their solution. **YITZHAK DANZIGER**

Danziger's first efforts were compact sculptures in stone which radiated strength and power. Their surfaces were smooth, and the light slid slowly across their clearly defined contours. The young Danziger immersed himself in the values of ancient Near Eastern sculpture and succeeded in

149

introducing into his own work the monumentality of the best sculpture of the past. That quality was equally evident in his new work, following a stay of several years in London. Now, however, he has given up stone for clay, plaster and welded iron.

Some time passed before he abandoned figuration altogether, and in that interim period he continued to fashion people and animals — *The Archer: Sheep*. The tranquil motionlessness of his stone figures yielded occasionally to dynamic restless forms expressive of the baroque. Some of his forms are more calm with only the hint of restrained movement (the turn of the sheep's head, for example) expressed through vigorously executed surfaces. This is equally true of his abstract works.

His dynamism finds full expression in *The Burning Bush* with its single dominant form, and its many recurrent secondary ones. Here he uses large cylindrical segments, sections of curved iron, which even in their unworked state, enclose space. *The Burning Bush* is among the first of a series of welded iron sculptures on which Danziger is at present engaged. It is an arresting representation of frozen fire with iron flames soaring heavenward. An emblem of fire and of growth and of the desire to rise — it symbolises the revelation and purpose of the burning bush.

Some of his sculpture is geometrical, constructed almost entirely of verticals and horizontals, with emphasis on one or the other. This work is endowed with powerful energy and decision by the careful positioning of the iron plates which establish incontrovertible facts by cutting through space. Other works are restless, being the sculptural equivalent of outbursts and agitations. They may consist of amalgams of straight smooth simple plates; or curved segments with tension implied in their unworked state.

The foundations of the soldiers' memorial at Holon, *Yad La-Banim,* consists of sections of long iron cylinders. These are the essential simplicity of a single form on which are based the cross-section variations which comprise the entire work. The metal cuts through the air, establishing the boundaries of the memorial and activating space, which constitutes a component no less richly expressive than the metal itself. This work has both movement and repose united in a muted cry and wordless pride.

In his latest creations in bronze, cast from wax, Danziger shows an instinctive

150

feeling for form which is in equilibrium despite its impetuousity. In his hands, the soft wax becomes a medium infused with tension by the slack sheets which he splits, tears and bends to render its two dimensions three. The resultant sculpture is a hollow mass embodying a controlled movement of light and air, which are subtly enveloped in sheets of bronze. During his years abroad, Danziger also essayed landscape architecture. His experience in that direction strengthened the bond between his sculptures and the area around them, giving him a special advantage in the design of monuments. His entire work is distinguished for the clarity of its line and form; there can be no mistaking his meaning, which he evokes vigorously and with superb confidence.

For many years Yehiel Shemi worked on solid monumental figures in wood, stone or clay. In these he emphasised volume and mass and paid particular attention to surface textures and the qualities peculiar to his various media. YEHIEL SHEMI

In the mid-1950's he began to work in welded metal. His first attempts were with figures, mostly of animals, constructed of thin sheets of iron welded together to form the sides of hollow figures. He wished, evidently, to merge his material with space, and to justify the hollowness of his creations by their apparent weightlessness. Some of his work is transfixed by ladder-like objects, from which the figures are suspended. This sets up two tensions — a feeling of weight contrasted with weightlessness and of solidity against space.

Other works consist of amorphous leaves or sheets of metal which counterbalance the surrounding space by their curves and their attachment to metal staves, which altogether form a composition of line and surface. From that period onwards, space became an integral part of his sculptural thought.

In this later sculpture which has remained figurative despite a high degree of stylisation, Shemi sometimes uses scrap-metal and spare machine parts which thus acquire new meaning and an organic character. He preserves the texture of the metal, using its jaggedness, its roughness, and the marks of welding and solder, to strengthen the impression of organic growth.

More recently he has worked in a more restrained fashion, limiting himself to abstractions in which geometric form predominates. An entire series of these consists of iron disks attached to each other in a balanced manner, almost without movement, and with emphasis on right angles and the dominance of vertical or horizontal in any one piece.

After a stay in Paris, the present phase of his work is a kind of synthesis of spontaneity and discipline. Wires placed in parallel formations cre te the illusion of a plane which contrasts with the material surface of the metal plates and heightens the illusion of volume in space.

His principal medium today is iron plates, rectangular and convex, made to seem more natural by the untouched effects of welding. This quality of nature, together with a movement in the compositions themselves, endow these pieces with a great feeling of spontaneity and animation, and bring them into a direct relationship with the natural free sculpture of his first work in iron.

DOV FEIGIN Dov Feigin, after years of work in stylised solid stone and clay, has now adopted welded metal as his principal medium. In the beginning he created the effect of solid masses as he had in stone and clay by closely welding plates to give the impression of solid form. But in time he gave up masses, and like many another who has turned to metal, abandoned closed solid volumes for open ones of outlined space, enclosed in the air as it were, by a metal framework.

Feigin then began to make metal drawings in space; linear drawings sometimes staved together to form two-dimensional surfaces, to produce a play of forms and an open construction uniting the metal sculpture with the space around and within it. These sheet areas are sometimes constructed as networks of straight wires which together form planes.

An illusion of two dimensions is thus created by single-dimensional lines; and the building-up of these in varying positions produces the further illusion of spatial volume, and three-dimensional objects. These forms charge with tension the air enclosed by the metal wire.

Flexibility and a feeling of being able to breathe are thus imparted to the medium, rather in the way that the ribs induce a similar feeling of strength and freedom in the human frame.

Despite the abstraction of his work, it lacks geometric coldness, and possesses

152

an organic feeling like that of a growing plant, which gradually grows taller, now and then brings forth a new leaf, and yet never loses a sense of unity at each stage of its growth. Feigin's sculpture has the same sensations of continuity and growth; like plants it is typified by light and spaciousness.

The early work of Elul Kosso was distinguished by a meandering decorative line delineating the curves of stylised female figures, and he was at first most happy with wood as his medium. Later he acquired an expressionist technique, modelling in clay and wax. At this stage, he tried to rid himself of the decorative elegance of his earlier work; his style became, in consequence, more temperamental. Moving gradually towards abstraction, he began to use leaves of metal, torn or bent to give an added dimension. In this manner he introduced space into his compostions, with distorted holes in the leaves. Despite his emotionalism, a characteristic elegance is still an integral part of his work. Space, previously regarded by him as dynamic, since it was created by tearing the edges of the metal, became more static, imprisoned by the holes pierced in the material.

Despite their abstract quality and near-geometric form, his sculptures appear like living organs — eyes and mouths — or even as wounds in the living body. They seem, too, to be in movement, eyelids and lips opening and shutting; wounds on the point of closure; and this is the source of their vitality and power.

The play of light and shadow upon these hollows and cracks endows them with vitality. The erotic flavour of his earlier figures is now replaced by a brutal, coarse tearing of the body, in an effort to give it a fresh primordial character without resorting to the decorative charm of the earlier pieces.

David Palombo is not satisfied with the traditional media of wood and stone; not only does he supplement these with welded metal, but also with glass; and uses several materials combined in a single piece. However, he is always careful to match medium and subject.

He favours solidity in stone, simple in its closed natural form, and rarely breaking it down into smaller parts, or juxtaposing a number of large forms. In wood, also, he favours solidity; sometimes he works through large, quiet planes which reveal the beauty of the grain; sometimes his treatment is quasi-natural, with the branches and trunk of a tree left in their original form, twisting and acquiring shape and direction in the earth, interspersed with shadows and crevices.

His technique is quite different with welded metals. He creates illusions of growth, and makes structures in space using metal rods, sometimes soldered to create planes, sometimes welded together to give an impression of organic forms conjoined by chance. They are roughly finished, with traces of the welding in evidence, which intensify the impression of chance, disorder, and lack of polish to which contemporary sculptors seem to be partial.

He uses glass as an amorphous mass coagulated by heat, and sometimes carves it as he would stone. He rarely uses glass by itself, but employs it to contrast with or complement another material.

Though his treatment varies with the material, his works have some qualities in common. His materials are left to display their natural properties, and his forms are organic and seemingly fortuitous. They are, despite appearances to the contrary, carefully controlled. Sometimes he uses a natural form as the basis for a piece. In this sense, Palombo belongs to the international group of sculptors and painters which considers itself bound by nature, even when working in what appears to be the abstract.

These artists practice a new kind of naturalism; not one of figures, ideas and narratives, but of forms, textures and organic materials. This new naturalism has its origin in the baroque spirit of our generation. It comes to the forefront, for example, of those of Palombo's sculptures which he does not set on a stand or plinth, but which hang by a strand to swing with every puff of wind or light touch of the hand. Some are actual mobiles made of parts which move individually; others are non-mobile in intention but are hung by all-but-invisible wires in space, so that they seem to be closed bodies floating in air.

YIGAL TUMARKIN Yigal Tumarkin has been discussed elsewhere in this book as a painter. Because of the unique nature of his sculpture, however, some additional remarks must be made in this chapter. He collects objects and pieces of scrap metal, and assembles them into unified pieces. He tries to preserve the sharpness and hardness of iron while emphasising its physical nature; but by working it into special textures he creates the appearance of other materials. In the art of assembling scrap metal he always preserves a sense

154

of the former uses of the cast-off objects. It is not by chance that many surrealists have chosen the *objet trouvée* as a means of expression; and indeed Tumarkin's assemblages smack of surrealism.

His work expresses a cry of pain, a challenge to and a protest at comfortable, conventional society, in which the cast-off fulfilled quite other tasks. Disengaged from their former milieu, they evoke a feeling of imbalance: and belong to a new world of reality with unfamiliar rules and practices of its own. With these found objects, to brutal handling, Tumarkin succeeds in conveying his harsh message.

Like other countries, Israel has fewer sculptors than painters. The art of sculpture is more cumbersome, harder to master, and less rewarding than the art of painting. It lacks, at least to the same degree, the element of colour which is so expressive of the emotions. The charm, pleasure and sensuousness of colour make it one of painting's most powerful weapons. Using colour alone, a painter can involve a viewer in a picture and carry him along without that viewer being involved in essentials at all.

This is impossible in sculpture. A sculpture stands revealed before the beholder, any superficiality of thought or superfluity of material marring its compactness and conciseness, and allowing the virtuoso no opportunity of guile or concealment. Before a sculptural idea can be realised, the original plastic concept must be completely thought out, summarised, and stripped to its essentials. There is no avoiding these preliminaries. Here is the problem; and here the challenge confronting the would-be sculptor. Only a distinguished few accept that challenge. The elements which contribute to the strength of sculpture are also those which create its most formidable difficulties, and which account for the scarcity of sculpture and sculptors of the first quality. In addition, these same problems affect the public, who in Israel as elsewhere, are remote from sculpture, or worse, indifferent to it.

To all this, which has made sculpture one of the most painful of paths for the contemporary artist, must be added the obstacles peculiar to the siting of a statue in street or park. The atavistic rejection of the human figure, which stems from the Jewish attitude towards idolatry, is present still in many Jews. Alienated from visual expression, and educated only in the word, in written and spoken language, the People of the Book wanted no statuary in our cities and public places. For many years, the collective villages, and not many of those, were the only places where statues could be seen.

The necessity to raise memorials to the dead of the War of Liberation stimulated memorial sculpture, and from the early 1950's a new feature has appeared on the Israeli scene. Many of the monuments were restricted to architectonics alone; but the widespread construction of new buildings, — for example the Hebrew University and Haifa Technical College — has also stimulated the interest in sculpture, although even now, in national and municipal commissions, reliefs rather than free-standing forms are still the dominant type.

In the large cities practically no memorials have yet been erected. The few that exist were restricted to animal forms — for example, the lions in Ramat Gan by Hannah Orloff. In Tel Aviv, the biggest city in Israel, one free-standing monument has been built, the memorial to the pilots who defended the city, by Benjamin Tammuz, in the Gan Ha'atzmaut (Independence Park). Tel Aviv's second memorial, to the liberators of Yaffo, is a relief tablet by Kara, and similar to that by Priver in memory of the founders of the city. Only recently with the building of the Tel Aviv Exhibition Gardens have some statues been commissioned. In Haifa there are several animal figures in the park. Jerusalem is a problem peculiar to itself, and some considerable time will apparently have to elapse before the situation there improves.

Our sculptors are also hampered by the absence of any law making it obligatory to allocate a certain proportion of building expenses for artistic decoration.

A partial solution to the problem is provided by the tendency toward abstraction of many of our artists. Though abstraction is far from being appreciated by the larger part of the Israeli public, and conflicts with the taste of most patrons, yet it has been adopted by many as a way of solving the graven-image problem, and sometimes constitutes a pre-requisite in memorial competitions.

108. AHARON MELNIKOV.
MONUMENT TO THE HEROES OF TEL-HAI,
STONE 1926.

109.   BATYA LISHANSKY, PORTRAIT, PLASTER.

110. YAAKOV LUCHANSKY. PORTRAIT, ARTIFICIAL STONE.

111. ARYEH MERZER. BEATEN COPPER.

112. HANNAH ORLOFF. MONUMENT TO DOV GRUNER, BRONZE, RAMAT-GAN. ▶

בלהב המרד ...

113.   AHARON PRIVER. MOTHER AND CHILD, STONE.

114.   ZEEV BEN-ZVI. PORTRAIT, ARTIFICIAL, STONE,   ▶

115. RUDOLF LEHMANN. HERON, WOOD
Y. TSAFRIR COLLECTION TEL-AVIV.

116. RUDOLF LEHMANN. BIRD PLASTER. ▶

117.   RUDOLF LEHMANN. TORSO PLASTER.

118.   RUDOLF LEHMANN. BIRD, WOOD.

RUDOLF LEHMANN. GOAT, WOOD.

120. DAVID PALOMBO. GATE TO "YAD VASHEM" BUILDING JERUSALEM.

121. ARYEH REZNIK. HERON, WOOD.

122.   MOSHE STERNSCHUSS. BULL, WOOD.

123.   MOSHE STERNSCHUSS. WOMAN, ARTIFICIAL STONE.

124.   MOSHE ZIFFER. WOMAN WOOD, TEL-AVIV MUSEUM

125.   MOSHE STERNSCHUSS. MITSPE RAMON, 1962

126. MOSHE ZIFFER. COMPOSITION, WOOD.

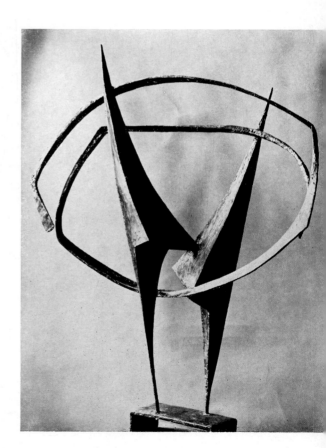

127. DOV FEIGIN. NEST, WELDED IRON.

128. DOV FEIGIN.
COMPOSITION IN WELDED IRON.

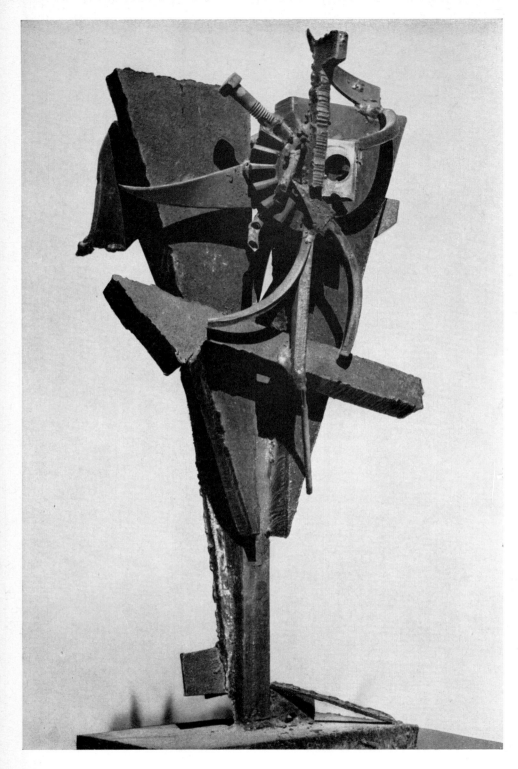

129. YIGAL TUMARKIN. FIGURE, IRON SCRAPS.

130. DOV FEIGIN. MITSPE RAMON, 1962.

131. ELUL KOSSO. COMPOSITION IN WELDED IRON.

132. ELUL KOSSO. COMPOSITION IN WOOD, YUGOSLAVIA.

133. YEHIEL SHEMI.
COMPOSITION IN WELDED IRON

134.   YEHIEL SHEMI. NEST, WELDED IRON.

135.   YEHIEL SHEMI. OWL, IRON SCRAPS.

136.   YITZHAK DANZIGER. NIMROD, DETAIL.

137.   YITZHAK DANZIGER. NIMROD, SANDSTONE.   ▶

138.   YITZHAK DANZIGER. THE EARLY RAIN, BRONZE.

139.   YITZHAK DANZIGER. MONUMENT TO FALLEN SOLDIERS "YAD LABANIM" IRON, HOLON.   ▶

140.   YITZHAK DANZIGER. SHEEP, PLASTER, "ISRAEL" GALLERY, TEL-AVIV.

141.   YITZHAK DANZIGER. THE BUSH, WELDED IRON. ▶

142.   YITZHAK DANZIGER. NEGEV, BRONZE, "ISRAEL" GALLERY, TEL-AVIV.

143.   RUTH TSARFATI. PORTRAIT ARTIFICIAL STONE.   ▶

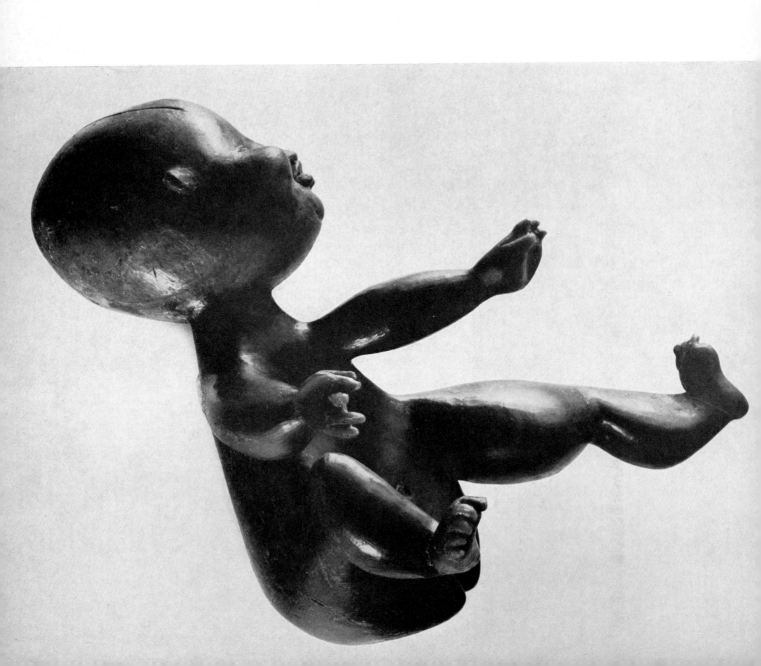

145. RUTH TSARFATI. GIRL, ARTIFICIAL STONE.

144. RUTH TSARFATI. INFANT BRONZE.

146. SHOSHANNA HEIMANN. TWO FIGURES, WOOD.

147. SHOSHANNA HEIMANN. THREE FIGURES, WOOD.

148. BENJAMIN TAMMUZ. MONUMENT TO FLIERS CONCRETE AND STAINLESS STEEL. INDEPENDENCE PARK,
TEL-AVIV. (ARCHITECT: ABBA ELHANANI; CONSTRUCTOR: PROF. HEINRICH NEUMANN).

149. SHAMMAI HABER. MEMORIAL, ATOMIC REACTOR NAHAL RUBIN. ▶

150.   HAVA MEHUTTAN. FIGURE, WOOD.

151.   HAVA MEHUTTAN. SPECTATORS ARTIFICIAL STONE.   ▶

152. HAVA MEHUTTAN. FIGURE ARTIFICIAL STONE.

ARCHITECTURE
AVIAH HASHIMSHONY

FOUR: ARCHITECTURE by AVIA HASHIMSHONI

Israeli architecture is a recent phenomenon only a few decades old, and is still far from having a clear-cut character of its own, for a composite art like architecture needs some time to achieve individuality and independence. Architecture springs not only from the inner world of the creator but is also dependent on the world in which it grows, and is subject to external pressures by that world.

However, the relationship between artistic expression and its native culture is not peculiar to architecture. Through his sensitiveness and perception, the artist gives expression to his cultural milieu, penetrating beneath the conventional expression of that culture, laying bare the true character of contemporary events, and even revealing the first signs of future developments. In architecture, indivisibly linked as it is with man's environment, this expression is particularly striking. The intimacy of the relationship between architecture and the general cultural fabric is the main reason why architectural expression attains clarity but slowly. In order to arrive at clear artistic expression, the creator must be free, not only to express himself, but to choose the means by which he expresses himself. To us today it is obvious that a basic necessity for the surprising artistic achievements of our time is the freedom won for art about a century ago (even if, when breaking with tradition and desire for innovation itself became traditional, that freedom may appear as a negative rather than a positive quality).

The freedom of the architect is limited in two special ways; first in the close relationship between himself and whoever is to make use of his creation, that is, his client; secondly between himself and the executors of his plan, that is the builders, the craftsmen and technicians. These two factors lacking the directness, the freshness, and the rooted certainty which were the heritage of historical architecture, nevertheless enter the creative process and modify the general pattern of spontaneous construction.

The client appears in many guises. He is the man who uses the building, the citizen who passes it, the visitor who admires it. All these have to be able to see the building as part of their own environment. The client is the administrator assigned to oversee some municipal housing project. The client is the Town Planning Officer or the Borough Engineer who has to determine the character and extent of a construction, and is the authorised representative of the tens of thousands of people who will use the architect's creation. He sometimes regards himself as the one responsible for the creation.

In this event, the lack of direct contact between the architect and the people who will use his building creates a situation in which the artist's professional and creative responsibility to his client has dwindled to almost nothing. It has been assumed by an administrator whose technical knowledge and cultural background seldom allow him to act like the patron or connoisseur of earlier times.

A similar situation exists between the architect and the builder. Construction today is passing from the hands of the craftsmen to the machines and factory-hands. This has immeasurably increased the importance of the building contractor who economically controls construction methods. Consequently the former intimate relationship between the artist-architect and the worker-craftsmen who gave body to his notions has weakened.

This state of affairs is peculiar to our time. On the one hand, the architect cannot extend his activities beyond the walls of his studio and consummate an independent creation which mirrors his inner vision; on the other, no basis of understanding has yet been reached between client and builder, allowing them to advance architecture behind the scenes, as it were. The position is not wholly unfavourable to the architect, however. While the influence of client and contractor has increased in the past fifty years, the importance of the architect's public role has also increased. In some places now, no building at all would be considered without prior consultation with an architect. The main reasons for this development are: first, that new forms of organised dwellings on a large scale, large multi-purpose public buildings, cities designed to fulfil many different purposes, and the transfer of a large part of daily activities from the private domain of the family to the public one of the town, the city and the state are beyond and outside the scope of ordinary citizens, craftsmen, even engineers. The services of the architect are required as an artist able to design new forms, and evolve systems of organization to include both living and working areas of any given society.

Secondly, that an historical examination of the past and present natures of civilization has proven the need for an aristic component in the life of society. Such a component in the present eliminates the need to depend on the art of the past.

These two conditions have brought about a shift of emphasis in the architect's role. Contemporary architecture constitutes a new realm of art which encompasses all man's building activities. The architect has ceased to be a talented but passive interpreter of the demands of consumer and contractor and attempts to shape a pattern of living for the former and to direct the activities of the latter.

Architecture's new role in society provides a useful frame of reference for a survey of Israeli architecture. The fifty-year-old Israeli school of architecture developed during that period when the profession of architect took on this broader meaning of which we have written. It is an integral part of general contemporary architecture, paralleling its growth, experiments, and achievements.

As a style fashioned by a new society in a new land, and within a newly emerging social, economic, political and even demographic framework, Israeli architecture at the outset was devoid of all traditions. Consequently, it borrowed its guiding principles and techniques from analogous but heterogeneous schools of contemporary architecture. It is important to consider the effect of local factors on these imported principles, and at the same time to trace the ways in which these principles were themselves altered by Israeli architects as they attempted to adapt them to their own styles.

Planning ideals in these early years sometimes came into conflict with the need to find the appropriate physical expression for new social structures like the *kibbutz* and the *moshav;* with mass housing for new immigrants first through private builders and later through land settlement agencies; with limited budgets; and with the formation of experimental cadres of craftsmen and builders while work systems and techniques were being perfected.

The planners were inspired by such Utopians as the Englishman Sir Patrick Geddes, the Frenchman Toni Gernier, and the American White, and by a subsequent generation which included Le Corbusier and Alexander Klein. All these men strove to restore harmony to the living environment appropriate to contemporary society. This ideal of planning, which also appeared in the works of Theodore Herzl and other Zionist Utopians, such as Elhanan Leib Levinsky and Boris Schatz, exerted an especially strong influence on the first generation of architects. The second generation was raised on the idea of popular housing as a socialist ideal, and regarded that aspect of planning, and the *shikun* or housing project as the focus of its problems.

In addition to the conflicts outlined above, which ran counter to Utopian solutions, another factor much influenced Israeli architecture, that of Time. Most Israeli building to this day is still subject to the pressure of urgency and the need for swift planning without adequate preparation. Large-scale projects, public buildings, new towns and regional developments embracing both rural and urban areas are made in haste. Even over-all plans for nationwide building are produced under relentless pressure. It is no wonder then that given these conditions two types of architecture predominate. In one, improvisation plays a large part; the other is based on stereotyped formulae which fulfil only a small part of architectural requirements.

When we see how one distinct image has taken shape from so many diverse factors, we cannot but marvel at the power of contemporary architecture in developing as an artistic creation specific to our times; and at the intensity of Israeli architects' efforts to search for an independent form of expression after having solved the planning problems.

Before statehood and after, Israeli architecture can be divided into four phases, which by chance each cover a decade: phase one — up to 1920; phase two — 1920–30; phase three — 1930–40; phase four — 1940–50. We shall also discuss the two latter transition periods.

Phase One: The period which preceded the emergence of a specific Israeli architecture lasted from the middle of the Nineteenth Century to the end of World War I. It witnessed the first organised attempts by Jews in the Holy Land to establish rural and urban settlements. The following buildings belong to this period:

1. The first blocks of dwellings in Jerusalem, for example, in the Yemin Moshe and Meah She'arim districts, and in the living quarters of immigrants according to land of origin. For the first time, the influence of organised housing ideas which had developed in England were noticeable here.

2. Baron Edmond de Rothschild's villages, built by French settlement organisers according to a standard plan.

3. Independent villages such as Petah Tikva and Hadera, planned by German engineers of the Templar colonies.

4. The first residential areas of Tel-Aviv and Haifa, based on Mediterranean city models.

5. Public building of a tentative "Israeli" style, based on an eclectic combination of Eastern, Moslem and Assyrian elements, for example, Haifa.

Phase Two (1920–30):

The First Decade of Jewish architecture in Palestine saw the appearance of the following:

1. Eclectic constructions in the newly-developed residential parts of Jerusalem, Haifa and Tel-Aviv.
2. New types of rural communities — *kibbutz* and *moshav* settlements.
3. The first stages of contemporary functional building — the Jewish Agency and Hebrew Seminary buildings in Jerusalem, dining halls and children's homes in the *kibbutz* villages.

Phase Three (1930–39): This period was marked by the continual development of functional building especially after the pattern of Central European architectural trends; the development of urban housing, including various forms of council housing, and small apartment houses in a planned garden-city network; and the first attempts at neighbourhood projects and organised housing schemes based on traffic distribution.

Phase Four (1939–48): During this phase, building work was disturbed by World War II. In the short period of construction between 1944 and the establishment of the State of Israel in 1948, the values and principles of building of the previous phase were formalised. A pseudorustic style of Swiss architecture gained currency in building design.

The architecture of the British Mandate was then supplanted by that of the State of Israel. Israeli architecture as such may be divided into two periods, from 1948 to 1955 and from 1955 to the present. Between 1948 and 1955 particular attention was paid to apartment housing and to the problems of national planning; architectural ideas were those of the preceding phase, particularly in the influence of English satellite-town planning.

From 1955 onwards there was a marked tendency to look for new forms of comprehensive planning for all the components of a city — public buildings, housing, traffic regulation and a proper blending of working and residential areas. Southern architectural concepts originating in the French Midi and Latin America were applied with greater frequency and new Scandinavian trends began to exert a considerable influence.

The conditions in which Israeli architecture and the Palestinian architecture which preceded it had to operate are very different from one another. Israeli building needs are much more numerous and include the whole construction field — national planning, regional housing projects, factories and public buildings. Speed became paramount, for the population increased four-fold in fifteen years. New architectural opportunities offered themselves, for most building in Israel is carried on with public funds and generally is supported by law as well as by land policies. Under these conditions the special characteristics of the architecture of the most recent period evolved. Nor must we forget that the foundations of present day Israeli architecture are based on those of the Palestinian Jewish community. The period between 1948 and 1955 shaped the character of the Jewish population centres in town and country in places where nothing had previously existed. The architectural facts established at that time today supply a background of tradition, though whether we accept or reject that tradition is another matter. It is a short-lived and unusual tradition. It would be difficult to compare it with the long-established tradition of Europe, which slowly emerged from the Middle Ages onwards. Nor can it be likened to the briefer tradition of American architecture. Although the latter resulted from a transfer of European architectural forms to the New World, it incorporated many features deriving from local popular rural building. Palestinian Jewish architecture was formed through copying an urban architecture, the basic principles of which remained obscure.

In addition, spontaneous creation is almost entirely absent in the pre-State tradition, which employed rational planning as its basis. The functional approach and the desire for comprehensive planning were adapted to local conditions and adjusted to the modest scale of building of the pre-State period by the Israeli architect. Practical solutions and a lack of pretention typified that era.

Together with these features, we find excitement over the very act of building, a sense of public responsibility, and a relentless search for proper solutions to the country's unique building problems. The pre-State architect was conspicuous for his co-operative attitude toward the material requirements of building work, and sometimes identified his viewpoint with these demands to the stage where he would subordinate his plans to economic consideration and the demands of the client; and would relinquish his formal and schematic ideas when they conflicted with prevailing conditions. This situation often resulted in the erection of incomplete buildings which aroused criticism from those trying to perpetuate the Israeli tradition. The latter have sometimes resorted to extremes, particularly in recent years, which have been marked by a change in values with the advent of a clientele wishing to express affluence and power through the building it commissions. The architects of the previous decade would also try to ignore the 'tradition' altogether, instead of seeing it in its true perspective, that is, as a point of departure for a maturing and refinement of form. This form, despite its lack of cohesion and imperfections, is now being transformed in a direct and vital manner.

We divided the first period of Israeli architecture roughly into decades, and shall now consider in detail the special features of each phase.

The decade 1920–30 was distinguished by an eclectic architecture designed to create an Israeli-Zionist style which would serve as a model for the rebuilding of the Jewish State. The ideologist and teacher-in-chief of this trend was the architect Alex Berwald, who made his influence felt both through his own buildings, and through his position as first lecturer in architecture at the Hebrew Technion in Haifa.

ALEX BERWALD Berwald was a Jewish architect from Germany who was invited to design the Reali secondary technical school and the Technical College at Haifa before World War I. For this purpose he studied Moslem and Mediterranean architecture and attempted to achieve a synthesis between their outer forms and strictly functional interiors. Berwald discovered Arab builders with experience in working for the English, the French and the Germans. He learned their methods and familiarised himself with typical buildings in old Haifa and on the coast. Because of his exceptional talent, and his active identification with the formal and technical values of his new surroundings, he succeeded in erecting buildings which, despite their eclecticism, possess positive qualities.

Notwithstanding Berwald's extensive influence, it became apparent that

206

apart from small-scale town building the eclectic approach could not serve as a basis for the architecture of a new country, since it was no more than an attempt to force old buildings into new forms, and to give the appearance of novelty by using new materials such as reinforced concrete. Slowly the ideas of contemporary architecture began to penetrate that of Jewish Palestine, and Berwald himself in the last works he carried out before his untimely death in 1931, hinted at changes in his attitude and doubts concerning the direction he had formerly taken.

The views of the modern planning school became an important factor in the creation of the new collective and co-operative settlements, particularly through the work of the architect Richard Kaufmann.

Kaufmann, like Berwald, came from Germany while still fresh to his profession, and versed in the new ideas of town planning which had been influenced by the British idea of the garden-city as the city of the future. This kind of thinking chimed well with Zionist ideals which not only advocated a return to nature and the pre-eminence of agriculture, but which also wished to exploit the achievements of science in the creation of the perfect state. In Kaufmann's time, and indeed for some time after, the garden-city idea seemed the most suitable for new cities anywhere in the world. Kaufmann was appointed to design most of the villages and garden suburbs established in the decade 1919–29. As a modern architect, he was free of eclecticism, and adapted his architectural solutions to the new concept of planning and to the technique of reinforced concrete. Kaufmann attained the position of pioneer town-builder for the entire country by his many years of prolific activity during which he planned a great many settlements, and suggested solutions for the basic problems of *kibbutz, moshav* and urban residential planning. He also designed many individual buildings. Those in the warmer regions of the country, for example at Deganya, and on the northern shores of the Dead Sea have aroused special interest because of the ways in which he exploited climatic elements in relation to contemporary tropical building. This experiment even harmonised with Kaufmann's aesthetic approach since in it he was able to combine rational planning with monumental design.

RICHARD KAUFMANN

207

His success in realising his planning ideals was attained with the support given him by the Jewish settlement authorities and especially by Dr. Arthur Ruppin, at that time a key figure in these activities. This is a good example of the influence that can be exercised on the development of architecture by an intelligent and farsighted client. At the same time, however, there was an ideological conflict raging between Kaufmann's attitude and that of the majority of architects working in this country; so that his pioneering work was not resumed by others until the third phase of Israeli architecture. This happened after Kaufmann's retirement and the cessation on his part of developing his technique. Eclectic architecture had already lost its place, and the overall number of architects, particularly those trained in concepts similar to those of Kaufmann, had increased.

The progress of pre-State architecture, from eclecticism and the desire to create a local style based in practice on a full understanding of the underlying principles of architecture, is dramatically exemplified in the 1927 competition for the design of the National Institutions Building in Jerusalem. This building or rather group of buildings was to represent the headquarters of a state in the making. The judges included the Viennese Jewish architect, Joseph Frank. The plan chosen was that of an architect almost unknown at that time, Yohanan Ratner. Contrary to views popularly held at the time, Ratner's plan neither included any historical element, nor did it follow the monumental symmetry which characterised nineteenth-century architecture.

His plan, which was analytical and functional, envisaged a group of independent structures centred about a single hub, and built with outside walls of Jerusalem stone, the constructional framework and the interior walls to be of reinforced concrete. The plan received special praise for its success in emphasising clearly the function of architectural space as the inner content of architecture. It must be remembered that, in the period under discussion, the trend had shifted from building stylised structures to local patterns, and the influence of functionalism was gaining ground. The latter aimed at designs evolving from a sort of inner necessity, dictated by the function which any given building was required to fulfil.

Functionalism confronted the modern architect with a difficult problem of design. Since the architect had assumed the task of organising structural mechanics and of determining building techniques, he had no alternative but to transform these factors into decorative values of a distinctly arbitrary character. Conversely, Ratner's plan provided a new and different solution. Configuring the whole building complex with its surroundings, and creating a single plastic composition which encompassed all the component parts of the complex, he had produced a positive plastic value which simultaneously included all planning considerations.

This is a method which demands of the architect full control of his analytical skills and his abilities as a plastic artist. Ratner's approach was rejected, however, by nearly all Israeli architects, not only because they were unable to accept its ascetic nature, and its lack of imitable elements; but also because of the nature of the large-scale building activity in the 1930's following the new wave of immigration.

These immigrants came from Europe, chiefly from Germany. The architects of their buildings were themselves mostly young immigrants. New architects increased greatly in this decade — some were Israelis who had gone to Europe to study; some had acquired their professional education at the Technion under Berwald and Ratner; the majority, however, were skilled and even some famous architects who immigrated to Palestine from Central Europe and brought with them a backlog of experience in Middle European functionalist trends.

The architecture of the transition period 1928–1932 also deserves attention. This was a slack period in new building, especially in the cities. In the recently established agricultural settlements, however, the Arab riots of 1929 caused the re-canalisation of money towards constructional ends. At that time several interesting buildings of significance in the development of Israeli architecture were erected.

English architects working in Palestine followed their own stylised line of development. Harrison put up the small police stations in various parts of the country with a mixture of details from Arab and Cycladic architecture, and also planned the pretentious buildings of the Rockefeller Museum and the High Commissioner's Mansion in Jerusalem, this latter in co-operation with the perfectionist Winter.

Haikin built the Strauss Health Building in Jerusalem; Holiday the Scottish Church; Ratner the first wing of the Jewish Agency buildings. Berwald, in the period just before his death planned the first Sick Fund Hospital in Afula, and together with Ratner, the clinic on Rehov He-Halutz in Haifa, two buildings in which he exchanged the eclectic approach for the functional. Kaufmann erected the workers' housing group on the north shore of the Dead Sea.

LEOPOLD KRAKAUER

Leopold Krakauer became celebrated in this period on account of his buildings in *kibbutz* villages. He researched deeply in order to adapt the formal values of functional architecture to local conditions of climate and light. Krakauer dealt sensitively with the details of his building, regarding them as keys from which the entire structure developed. The decisive details of Krakauer's architecture are precisely those related to its function and to local conditions, such as the special arrangement of ventilators, the planning of gardens next to houses, the use of local materials in new ways.

The architecture of this first interim period summarised and crystallised the experiments of the previous decade, and had a significant though not exclusive influence on the continuing development of pre-State Palestinian architecture. Most of the architects of this time, with the exception of Berwald, who died in 1931, continued working for many more years; and some are active to this day. In the decade which followed, one marked by increased building demands, the need for architecture with a common purpose and pattern emerged. Then a change came over the Israeli architect's attitude towards his profession. He began to prefer a single school of thought which could accommodate the personality and the capabilities of the average architect, as well as those of the brilliant one. He wanted to be ready to meet the challenge posed by the necessity to think out each and every project anew.

ERICH MENDELSOHN

During this time, the well-known architect Erich Mendelsohn was active in this country. Mendelsohn, one of the greatest figures of the contemporary

210

school, succeeded in bringing the dramatic expression of the new structure to the thick-walled architecture of Central Europe.

Despite their fine quality, the buildings designed by Mendelsohn are not alone sufficient to explain the extent of his influence. The explanation lies in his brilliant drawings in which he presented his buildings as plastically emotive compositions unrelated to the scale of the actual buildings or the real degree of their impressiveness. His influence reached Jewish Palestine by a number of routes: by way of the younger generation of Israeli architects brought up on Herman architectural literature; by Mendelsohn's own publications; by the many architects who came to Palestine from Central Europe after having worked there according to concepts shaped by his thought; by works architected by himself in this country, several of which, for example the Haifa Hospital, constitute his crowning achievements.

Mendelschn's association with Israeli architecture began in 1925, when he was invited to design the first electric power stations. His most important activities were between 1934 and 1937, when he designed and supervised a series of public, commercial and apartment buildings. His views on architecture were not those of the fanatic and extremist, characteristic of such great architectural theorists as Le Corbusier, Gropius or Lloyd Wright. They were, however, sometimes Utopian and dissociated from contemporary reality; and they also lacked the rootedness of such architects as the Dutchman Seuker, the Frenchman, Perret, or the German, Loos.

Mendelsohn's architecture was essentially a compromise between the traditional building of his age and the constructivist and planning values of the new school. It is still too early to evaluate the overall importance of Mendelsohn in disseminating modern architectural ideas throughout the world. Limiting our assessment to Palestine, we may point out that here he assumed the role of co-ordinator and unifier, drawing together the efforts of many Jewish architects and setting them upon a single common path.

The Mendelsohn school of Israeli architecture of the thirties and forties was a positive phenomenon in that it introduced uniformity into much architectural activity which before had been confused and at conflict within itself; but it was natural that such a development could not lead to the creation of works of the first importance, since it lacked Mendelsohn's own great plastic talents at bridging the gap between banal architectural values and the literary dramatization of constructivist considerations. The Mendelsohn school therefore constituted a single segment only in the sphere of creativity; a large and influential part, but one which in terms of cultural development was a kind of *cul de sac*.

Together with this school two other distinct groups may be discerned. One included Ratner and Krakauer, who were active in the 1920s, and Heinz Rau, who arrived here in the thirties. This group did not work together, and included men whose individual styles were at variance with one another, sometimes in the extreme. Nevertheless, typical of them all was their pursuit of architecture as an art, in accordance with their individual ideas, and without subjugating their personal convictions to the needs of material success or the erection of as many buildings as possible.

The other group which began to form in this period included Sharon, Rechter, Carmi, Neufeld and others. Its members had all been here in the twenties, and were already familiar with conditions both in town and country. They left Palestine for European schools of architecture in order to widen their knowledge, and returned to the great wave of construction in Tel-Aviv at the beginning of the thirties. Their personal familiarity with local conditions; their identification with the latest ideals of European architecture, especially those of the Bauhaus at Dessau; and their individual talent and sense of reality allowed them to arrive at workable solutions of contemporary problems. Undaunted by the need for planning living places in town and country, the modernisation of buildings in collective villages, and the first housing projects, the members of this group supported by the leaders of the labour movement just then coming into being, and with origins and spiritual background in common, swiftly established a position of importance.

It would be impossible to review Israeli architecture in the late twenties and early thirties without mentioning a practice which to a great extent determined the nature of Israeli building at that time. This was the custom

212

of frequent competitions. Hardly any public building was erected in this decade without the architect being commissioned by competition. The judges were usually Professor Alexander Klein and Professor Yohanan Ratner of the Haifa Technion. Their presence usually guaranteed high quality, encouraged competent young architects, and ensured an awareness of new ideas.

Typical creations of this period are primarily apartment buildings. These included a Tel-Aviv apartment house built on columns by Rechter, and its further development and consolidation by Carmi; a workers' housing complex Shikun Ovdim by Sharon and Neufeld; and apartment houses in Jerusalem by Krakauer and Rau. Ratner was less active in this field as he was preoccupied with teaching, and also had to fulfil undercover military duties with the defence force, Hagana. Nonetheless, he won two important prizes for architecture, though his winning plans were rejected by the clients in a manner no less common in Israel than elsewhere.

Israeli architecture from 1935 to 1945 was interwoven with unusual events which greatly limited construction work. First there were the bloody disturbances of 1936 to 1939, then World War II, which was immediately followed by the struggle with the British which ended in the War of Independence and the creation of the State of Israel.

In the little construction that was carried out in this period, several novelties appeared. There was a marked tendency to create more solid central masses by use of Cubist constructions without protuberances; and a greater integration between buildings and their surrounding gardens. Architects made much use, too, of sloping roofs, which forced them to tighten their ground plans. The sloping red roof was associated in the popular mind with a variegated climate — rain, foliage and sunshine — which expressed a longing for more northerly atmospheric conditions.

These novelties were not fortuitous, but sprang from a strengthening of an urban ideology based on the principles of the garden-city. This mood was especially influenced by the models of new residential buildings near Zürich, and the classicist approach of the Jewish National Fund's chief architect, Alexander Klein. But a practical consideration also dictated the widespread use of sloping roofs; this was the lack of metal and wood for roofing concrete buildings. Because of this, builders had to choose wall systems using fewer imported materials.

During this period, a change also occurred in the planning of urban apartments. A new type of small apartment, which efficiently exploited breezes and broadened the spatial areas involved, appeared, and ultimately dominated the scene, although its first signs were already evident in 1935.

We have surveyed the first period of Israeli architecture which covers the thirty years of the British Mandate in Palestine. The most significant architects who worked here in that period have been mentioned, as have the attempts to develop national and regional styles, and the forces which brought about a unified manner of building.

To summarise this Palestinian Jewish architecture, the body of work which laid the foundations for the State of Israel's architecture and which constitutes our architectural "tradition", we find that it was based on modern views of practical and functional architecture while at the same time attempting to adapt the European manner to local conditions.

The adaptation to local conditions was partly effected as a result of factors beyond the control of the architect and the city planner. For example, concrete was much used because it was very economical to do so; land purchase was restricted to certain areas by the Mandatory Government; emphasis on buildings for residential purposes, and a dearth of land for public building, led to the erection of apartment houses in towns on sites originally intended for individual houses in garden-city developments. A stereotyped practicality which typified most building in the pre-State period was the result. On the other hand, the building of this time reflected formal qualities which stemmed from the architects' conscious attempts to adapt their work to the special conditions of the country.

This attempt is particularly obvious when we observe the manner in which the pre-1948 architect handled the outer shell of his building, regarding it as a skin which had to accommodate the coastal breezes to add to the physical comfort in the hot weather. Extensive use was made of balconies which broke up the severely cubic form, but allowed use of every slight

214

puff of wind, as did facing the buildings lengthways towards the prevailing wind, or facing the buildings north in airless parts, to achieve the maximum shade. All these adaptations to climate paid no attention to the spaces between buildings, the relationship between streets, squares and gardens, or the overall planning of the structures built among them.

The consideration given to climatic conditions, coupled with similar preoccupations, accounts for the apparent divergence between the architect's attempt to assert plastic values, and the end-product. This kind of building revealed a contradiction between the artistic opinions the architect had acquired from contemporary thought, and his actual practice.

The central European trend emphasised functional planning which it believed gave practical effect to Le Corbusier's dictum that "a building is a machine to live in". In its designs this Central European school emphasised wall areas, as it had in Central Europe. The window apertures are, however, smaller than those of the large glass areas of Atlantic coast architecture (for example, the Netherlands) but larger than those in Italy or other Mediterranean countries.

The consequence of this combination of large wall spaces with medium-sized windows is a building shell combining its function of isolation with its constructional requirements. A similar attitude towards wall design is found also in the building of the pre-State period, much of which was developed by architects of Central European origin. (Central European trends are noticeable also in the early work of Le Corbusier, who later, under the influence of his teacher Perret, and after fully digesting West European building concepts, arrived at an entirely different means of designing walls). The influence of this school accorded well with Zionist aims of creating a bond between man and his natural surroundings, and reorganising society.

Another kind of influence was exerted by the English garden-city theorists. Their ideas grew as a counter to the forbidding and inhuman building in England at the time of the Industrial Revolution, and aimed at restoring nature to the realm of human habitation. These ideas established two basic concepts: — the first was to regard landscape as an intergal part of urban dwelling, and embraced not only gardens and trees, but subjected planning completely to topographical considerations. The second, stemming from the sociology of housing, envisaged large-scale planning within an organic framework for groups of different sizes. It stressed the organisation of small groups of houses which should constitute neighbourhood units, which in their turn would in sum be a town. The separation of these units by garden areas was the principal means by which nature was to be re-introduced within the confines of the city.

The influence of the garden-city school was considerable, and provided a scheme of planning, albeit not the best, where lush landscaping was a practical impossibility, and a scheme indeed contradictory to the social needs of a country of high immigration, requiring economical, mass building.

Despite its wide prestige, the influence of Western European (French, Dutch and Belgian) architecture was hardly felt at all. The modern architecture of those countries demanded new construction techniques and new materials. The Western European school maintained its contact with tradition through intellectual constructivism and rationalism from the heyday of French Baroque to the present. As a characteristic regional style, it did not begin to influence Israeli architecture until recently, with the elimination of boundaries between regional schools.

Today, now that regional schools have lost their distinctiveness, no affinity can be found between Israeli architecture and that of any other given country. Pioneering styles in international architecture are concerned with the work, theories and general attitudes of individual well-known architects. The various viewpoints are numerous, some bearing precise names — for example, Brutalism, Neo-Brutalism, Neo-Vitalism, Organic Architecture, etc. Basically, however, all can be considered under one of the three following main streams of thought, each of which finds expression in the work of certain Israeli architects: Neo-Constructivism; Organic Functionalism; Neo-Formalism.

Neo-Constructivism is a continuation of the Constructivism of an earlier generation. It accentuates the character of the materials used in a given structure, for instance when the skeletal structure itself is meant for installations such as lifts which are assuming a greater importance at the present time in building. This school has emerged from the work of architects from August Perret to Louis Kahn.

Organic Functionalism attempts to synthesise practical functionalism and the organic approach. Its underlying idea is to find a *Gestalt* of building planning and design which can constitute a fitting framework for human life — for the individual and for society. Typical of this trend is a striving for well-defined proportions in every aspect of architectural creation, and in all dimensions. Thus the designer is concerned with one of two alternatives — either to attach small units to each other until the aggregate of them becomes a single complex unity — for example, individual rooms joined to form a house, houses to form a city; or to break down an entity into smaller and smaller divisions — for example, partitioning off a large hall into smaller halls and rooms which appear to float in space, or a definition of total space of a building by division into proportional components. This approach favours apportioning the rooms and their functions first, and aggregating them into a unit of building later.

Formalism attempts to reach the same goals as Constructivism and Functionalism, but by means of an accentuation of the plastic qualities of a building. Formalists hold that if an architect uses his plastic sense as a basic standard, he will attain an architectural entity satisfying the demands equally of technical logic and function.

The layman not conversant with the problems of contemporary architecture could well be surprised by this variety of approaches. He certainly has grounds for being astonished by the indifference of many contemporary architects to the functions required of a building; and the lack of pleasure and harmony to be found in buildings of the past. However, one must not lose sight of the fact that civilisation is today in the throes of numberless conflicts. Economic, technical, practical and emotional factors are continually at odds with one another. It is no wonder, then, that the contemporary architect is principally concerned with finding a *modus operandi* which will allow him to weld this body of contradictory factors into a single homogeneous fabric.

The conditions for the present-day Israeli architect resemble those in many other countries. They are characterised by intensive construction of housing units and entire urban residential areas; the abandonment of traditional craft methods and a growing use of industry in building; the rise of the managerial class as clients and as the decisive authority for the owners and occupiers; a growing involvement of the government in building matters; in the initiation of legislation and the elevation of building to a concern of the first rank in a welfare state. All these conditions common to other countries, tend to weaken the specific character of Israeli architecture. However, some qualities developed in the early phases of the Palestinian tradition still exist, though they are not to be easily discerned. They are generally to be found beneath the external forms which have often been borrowed in whole or in part from the works of architects who wield considerable influence as "leaders" of schools.

At the beginning of the modern movement, the work of Behrens, Loos, Berlege, Perret and Lloyd Wright already enjoyed special prestige. In the 1920s Le Corbusier, Pelzig and Mies van der Rohe commanded attention, having perfected techniques of design appropriate to new technological developments and the requirements of modern building organisation. During the past decade, however, Le Corbusier's influence has increased, while that of Gropius, van der Rohe and Lloyd Wright has waned.

In our opinion, the works of Le Corbusier have special significance beacuse of his penchant for building in southerly, Mediterranean regions. This being so, his style merges with the long-standing influence on Israel of Mediterranean architecture. The work of Gropius and van der Rohe originated in northwest Germany; Lloyd Wright's is the plain architecture of the American Middle West. Le Corbusier derives inspiration from Mediterranean culture, which explains his influence in Brazil, the Midi and India, all warm regions.

Southern architecture makes its appearance not only in the works of Le Corbusier, where it is the result of an identification with Mediterranean culture, but also in the technique of other well-known architects, particularly in the United States. An idealisation of Islamic architecture appears in the writings of Lloyd Wright, and is prominently, if banally, reflected in the work of Stone.

A group of van der Rohe's pupils, headed by Philip Johnson, rejected their teacher's approach and made use of elements of Oriental and Moslem architecture in order to achieve accented plastic qualities or, as Johnson himself defined it, for the purpose of introducing excitement and surprise into contemporary architecture. The American architect Louis Kahn, with his values at once rational and poetic, has also gained considerable vogue.

This brief account of world architecture and architects is important for understanding the values in which the working Israeli architect is immersed and which he attempts to introduce into his day-to-day work.

Contemporary Israeli architecture reveals three trends which are the outcome of the work of the groups we noted in the earlier Palestinian period. First there are the architects who followed the beaten track. Their approach crystallised the generally accepted formulations of Palestinian architecture and adopted the views current in England in the building of new cities after World War II, and in housing projects in London, Zürich and elsewhere in North West Europe.

In the second group, Sharon, Idelson, Weinrob, Mansfeld and others continued with their building programmes. They worked together with many young architects employed in their large studios. This collaboration was marked by reciprocal influences. The young men continued to search for a design which would combine practical logic dictated by the conditions of the country with a plastic expression stemming from the decorative elements of non-representational painting. The use of new materials played an important part in their thought.

Rau and Ratner typified the third group. Each went his own way, continuing HEINZ RAU to design works which were out of the ordinary but consistent with his previously established artistic direction.

Heinz Rau began his work in Palestine in the mid-1930s. Although he is a product of the German functionalist school, his independent and penetrating ideas have prevented him from assuming the routine approach to modern forms, which combines interior and exterior space by the superficial use of transparent walls. Rau achieves this fusion instead by emphasising light and shade, by scrupulous attention to the formal unity of interior and exterior space, by the establishment of sophisticated relationships between a building and its surroundings, and by a direct approach to materials, construction and details.

Rau is a perfectionist. He strives for a clear approach and the precise handling of relations between details and mass. Highly-polished exteriors and exterior decoration have their importance for him, too.

YOHANAN RATNER Yohanan Ratner was born in Russia and educated in Germany. He first appeared on the architectural scene in Palestine in the 1920s. Elsewhere we have already described his contribution to the diffusion of modern architecture here. The roots of his work are nourished by the Renaissance, and by the new architecture of Central Europe. Russian artistic thought and the plastic values of landscape and light peculiar to Israel have determined the direction these twin sources have taken in his development.

In his recent work, Ratner continues to expand his ideas on the relationship between the organisation of life in buildings and its plastic nature. He designs his buildings as *continua* of functional and spatial relationships. In this way he avoids simplicity in building masses, and the use of architectural forms in a 'rhetorical' manner. Ratner interprets each form individually and links them together through a mutual architectural relationship; then relates the building as a whole to the landscape. He can accomplish this because of his firm grasp of architectural principles. Conversely, he subordinates the details of a building to the general concept of the structure's interior and does not treat them merely as applied art.

Ratner's approach to the overall design of a building, and his somewhat cursory attitude to the finish of details, are unconventional and somewhat puzzling even to many architects working in Israel, among whom they are a subject for debate and censure.

As we have noted, the activity of Israeli architects since independence has been energetic, extensive and continually pressed for time. The fruits of this activity may be viewed rather as a collective than an individual effort. We prefer, therefore, to survey this most recent Israeli architecture in terms

220

of function (houses, public buildings, communal projects) rather than in terms of its individual creators.

It is natural that in a country in which more than half the population arrived in the space of fifteen years, the problem of housing should be the central one for the architect. At the beginning, erection of living quarters in the State of Israel was based on the solutions already established in the pre-State tradition. But, since these solutions were found inadequate for the greatly increased population, ceaseless efforts have been made to develop housing programmes. Experiments in this direction are concentrated on designing new apartment houses and the organisation of integrated residential areas. The Israeli architect is particularly concerned with the following objectives:

1. A marked expansion of aparment house development and its simultaneous adaptation for more occupants.

2. A breaking up of the repetitive character of units of living space, and a re-organisation of the apartments in a manner conducive to active social relationships.

3. Siting the apartments near areas of greenery, in the form either of small courtyards or large squares.

4. The improvement of the appearance of the exteriors of buildings and the creation of valid plastic values for entire neighbourhoods.

Israeli apartments are of smaller area than project apartments in many advanced countries. In addition, their layout raises the difficult question of their suitability to local climatic conditions.

Many types of apartment have been developed by various architects. Immediately after 1948, the predominant type was a small one- or two-storey building consisting of two apartments. This kind of structure embodied the conflict between the former desire for garden-cities with each dwelling in a plot of its own, and the necessity for more living units in concentrated residential areas. This was followed by a type of mongrel building much used in new towns and in the residential parts of already existing towns. It was not long, however, before architects realised that this mass-produced dwelling was unsatisfactory in many ways. It neither met the needs of a heterogeneous social framework nor allowed the use

221

of modern technical methods. Even when architects spent talent and much effort in creating more pleasing designs for this type of building the result was monotonous. In the early 1950s a number of architects submitted proposals to build large blocks of apartments comprising living-units of the Le Corbusier type; for sections built in the orthodox manner — that is, four apartments to a house; and for divisions made up of larger apartment houses. Neither the housing ministry nor their architectural advisers considered these suggestions seriously.

Subsequent housing in Israel was based on oblong structures four storeys' high having four or six flats on each floor with a separate entrance and stairwell for each pair of flats. This was economically advantageous as it suited building techniques then in use in this country. Aesthetically, however, the results were less satisfying. The buildings were erected in parallel, with the spaces between them determined only by practical considerations of lighting and ventilation, with no opportunities for the architect to design the intervening spaces in a manner pleasing to the eye, and useful for such things as children's games, or outdoor activities.

Long parallel rows of flats have other practical disadvantages. Ventilation, so important in Israel's climate, is impaired when one block obstructs the free flow of air to its neighbour. The system also lacks flexibility and does not lend itself to variations in design and their adaptation to the physical and social requirements of occupants differing in family structure, income and social background. Of course these are not problems peculiar to Israeli architects alone; they exist wherever intensive residential development is a necessity. Everywhere attempts are being made to solve these problems through new methods of organising architectural landscape; and information as to solutions is being exchanged.

An incentive to the search for new architectural forms was provided by the *Interbau* building exhibition, held in West Berlin in 1958 (the earlier exhibition held in Berlin in 1927 also significantly influenced housebuilding design). The *Interbau* exhibition was designed as a self-contained residential district. Its various structures were planned by outstanding architects from different countries who were allowed an extraordinary degree of freedom

222

in their artistic endeavours. The buildings did not present startling novelties, but they did display practical examples of advanced ideas which had hitherto been unexpressed.

This exhibition stimulated the world's architects to greater efforts in search of new techniques, and the housing client (the administrator in charge) was presented with a practical example of a new cliché-free approach to apartment design. The Israeli architect, too, was moved to look for new solutions in housing construction. He was now possessed of sufficient building experience to allow him to handle his housing 'material' with a greater degree of control and therefore of freedom.

The aims of the new search were, in the technical sphere, exterior design and social planning, that is, architectural design as a framework for man's total cultural and social life. Several developments occurred in the progress of exterior design and social planning, which included a greater degree of freedom and enterprise in the spatial design of residential neighbourhoods; a wider variety of structures — low, medium and tall buildings, apartments of varying sizes; interesting experiments in the consolidation of housing based on the Le Corbusier "dwelling unit" concept; and a search for absolute relations between inter-structural space and the structures themselves, as opposed to the accidental and monotonous spacing between buildings in rows.

In terms of building design, a recent tendency has been to endow structures with an extreme sharply-defined exterior form, both in the shell and in the entire mass.

In the exterior surface design there have been many attempts to enrich the wall-textures by using bare concrete, but exploiting rhythmic protuberances of the structure, by a decorative arrangement of wall apertures, sometimes contrary to their practical use.

In the design of building mass, two contrary trends may be observed. One consists of increasing the proportions of mass in length or in height to attain an architectonic effect of "size"; the other also aims at an impression of powerful striking plasticity but through the use of daring constructional forms, accenting parts of the structure close to one another in a kind of

Baroque dramatisation of the whole building as a network of masses united by the design. This may be due to the dissatisfaction of an architect working principally in the field of apartment housing. Finding such commissions anonymous and without glamour, he seeks to project his personality through the use of large volumes, in this way attaining a monumentalism which, in previous generations, was achieved in public buildings.

The two formal qualities mentioned above, exaggerated proportions and the plasticity of masses, are to be found in more concise forms in the historical examples of wall-structures and fortified towns. Indeed, the influence of the "all-concept" in Israeli and in world architecture is quite amazing.

Following the example of other countries, three model housing complexes have been designed and constructed in Israel by groups of architects given varying degrees of freedom. The three are located in Ramat-Aviv near Tel-Aviv, Beersheba, and Ramat-Hadar, Haifa.

The Ramat-Aviv project was designed along more or less conventional lines with the accent on modern well-planned apartments and an harmonious juxtapostion of building groups. The apartment layouts are based on the tradition of apartment planning developed in Israel through the years, with various attempts to consolidate solutions, but without innovations.

The model housing project in Beersheba is different. Here an attempt was made to depart from the garden-city tradition and the in-town developments of Tel-Aviv, and to contrive an urban character by borrowing forms from desert Arab prototypes. In this scheme a new eclectic impulse found expression in the use of two forms of desert building typical of North Africa. One pattern follows the design of a vertical *kasbah* made up of many-storeyed buildings arranged as a fortress wall. The other is the horizontal *kasbah* composed of low, closely-arranged houses which spread out even on the streets.

The residential project in Ramat-Hadar was constructed under quite different topographical conditions from the other two, which were built on a flat terrain. Ramat-Hadar constitutes an isolated segment at the end of the horizontal thrust of the Carmel Range overlooking Haifa Bay. The general spatial organisation of the project resembles Italian peak construction; a ring of high buildings encircles the hill-top on which the public buildings are situated. This plan is based almost exclusively on the "housing unit" type — large blocks of flats, each of which is almost a suburb in its own right. Some of the buildings are of the vertical slab type while others are towers.

Apart from the concentrated and various experiments in model housing projects, numerous efforts indicate a search for fresh organisation of residential districts, and the inauguration of new types of dwelling. These include a considerable number of buildings with a central stairwell to allow a freer arrangement of inter-structure areas; attempts at organising apartment houses in meandering compositions to facilitate a continuity of spatial flow; and experiments in abandoning rectangles in horizontal levels in favour of a design which provides the spaces between buildings with the qualities of vertically enclosed architecture.

Public buildings also offer the Israeli architect considerable possibilities. Here, too, there is a tendency to erect large building complexes, such as the Government Centre (Kiryat Hamemshala) in Jerusalem, the campuses of colleges and technions in Jerusalem, Rehovot and Haifa, the Cultural Centre in Tel-Aviv, and others. Centres in towns founded since the establishment of the State were also planned as groups of buildings related to each other in a definite pattern.

The most striking example of a public building complex erected in Israel is that of the Hebrew University in Jerusalem. The overall plan was prepared by the architects Kaufmann, Klarwein and Rau, and the various buildings were each designed by different architects who were requested to conform to the overall plan.

The campus extends along the side of a long narrow foothill. Its main section consists of a group of faculty buildings the dimensions and proportions of which were determined by the master plan. Considerable attention was given not only to the planning of the buildings themselves, but also to the design of the streets, fencing, landscaping and open areas between the buildings. The results of this kind of approach are very satisfactory and indicate very clearly that concern for inter-structural space should be exercised when the buildings are going up, and not postponed till a later stage.

The buildings on the campus are of unequal quality as to form. Some seem to indicate that their designers were not entirely happy with the stone which is the obligatory building material in Jerusalem, and the results are sometimes buildings not best suited to execution in such material. The more perfect buildings are those which were free of this contradiction at the outset, for example, the Synagogue and the Archaeological Institute. Other buildings in which the architects accepted the discipline of the stone are the Mathematics Institute, and the Theatre, where stone slabs are an excellent medium.

The architectural character of the Haifa Technion is of yet another kind. The overall quality of this complex can not yet be determined, as the open areas are as yet untreated. On the other hand, the architects who designed the Technion were allowed great formal freedom within a fixed budget; the buildings are separate from each other, and located in clusters of pine trees.

The master plan was drawn up by architect and town-planner Alexander Klein, based on the precinct system. The general approach is of stern and rational distribution expressed through expertly implemented classical design principles. The freedom of design granted to the individual architects offers an opportunity of examining various approaches to composition.

In most cases, the composition is of a commonly accepted type, that is, the relationship between two complementary bodies. The slopes of the site also made it possible to enhance the buildings by compositions incorporating perpendicular perimeters and free design roofs. Several buildings in this complex are considered of great merit.

The Aeronautical Department building, the work of Rattner, shows a concise solution of the problems of functional spatial organisation. The relationship between Man and Edifice finds inspired expression in the approaches to the building; its entrance; the lines of movement between its component parts; and in the way in which its various functions are concentrated about a network of studies and passages. Here, again, Ratner

226

displays his ability to develop the functional aspect of a building simultaneously with spatial design.

The interesting buildings of Haifa Technion also include the students' dormitory, the prize-winning plan of which was drawn up in a competition, by Khavkin. Here the relationship of the individual to the entire building has been emphasised, and to that end some individual comforts have been sacrificed. The general solution recalls Le Corbusier. On the smaller scale of the dormitory, this solution is more equable than in its application to large buildings where the end result seldom justified such humanistic pretensions.

In our survey of Israeli architecture we have tried to focus attention on the central problem, that of establishing a proper proportion between planning for the individual and planning for the anonymous public. In between these two extremes, there is an intermediate area in which the individual comes into contact with the small group. In this area relationships are subject to chance and difficult to define.

The new understanding of the importance of this factor — the small social group — in architecture is expressed in various ways. On the one hand, designers try to emphasise the aesthetic qualities of building masses which shall avoid banality and to create centres of interest which shall add variety to the urban landscape. This emphasis may be criticised when it is not based on an analysis of real needs. On the other hand, a solution is posited by the creation of several types of dwelling and public building in a single complex, where an attempt is made to express various group needs in the social structure.

Special notice must be given to the growing importance attached to relating a building to its surroundings, that is, the need for a bond between the architect's creation and the circumambient light, air and landscape. With this approach, natural surroundings become an integral part of the architectural creation and constitute a link between the individual and the group. In order fully to present the architectural values either of a single work or of the work of a whole country, as this survey attempted, a literal description or even one fully documented with photographs is insufficient, and can be misleading. A proper grasp of the subject can only be secured by seeing the buildings and gaining direct impressions of their scale, details and relationship to their environment. Only in this way can the artistic merit and special attributes of Israeli architecture properly be gauged.

We are prompted to ask ourselves if Israeli architecture exists on its own or as a distinct style. It is a reasonable question, since we associate the concept of style with a sureness of consistent creation free of futile gropings; but equally we used to associate the concept of style with such factors as special design requirements of parts of buildings, and especially with external decorative elements.

The tendency to create a style by the deliberate use of decorative elements is not at all new. Ever since the Renaissance, there have been long periods of time in which superficial manifestations derived from a literary or romantic decorative approach have been accepted in the place of a true style. Therefore, when we ask ourselves whether Israeli architecture has reached a maturity of artistic style or not, we must first determine whether we mean by 'style' a certain sophistication of decorative externals or style as comprehensive planning and design.

An examination of stylistic manifestations shows that many recent works by Israelis display decorativeness. But since these Israeli architects are students of the practical modern school, this decorativeness is expressed in pseudo-constructivism in which various buildings are divorced from simplicity and directness by the almost systematic use of forms borrowed from larger and industrially-fabricated structures. This accounts for the use of rhythmical repetitions, natural to large buildings in industrial centres, on small buildings; the use of walls with huge openings for small buildings; forms derived from prefabricated techniques on ordinary buildings; dramatisation of structural and spatial frames out of proportion to the building's content.

In terms of the development of Israeli architecture, these manifestations, to be found also in the work of many other world-famous architects outside Israel, are undesirable, and constitute a fashion destined to pass. It is to be hoped that this practice will leave behind it, however, a desire for formal completeness which is its only justification.

The true values of architecture in Israel are not to be measured, however, by the decrees of fashion, the profusion of decoration, nor the belittlement of formal values in some works. The special quality of Israeli architecture is to be found in the breadth of planning and organisation, in the principle of comprehensive building direction; in conforming to a scale for people living in surroundings new to them; in the practical approach to the solution of architectural problems.

The defects, but also the merits, of Israeli architecture stem from the fact that its well-spring is not greatness but vitality. Only a few creations have succeeded in synthesising greatness and vitality; the majority indicate that architecture in Israel is still in the process of crystallisation.

SQUARE,
END OF 18TH CENTURY,
ACRE.

154. MEAH SHEARIM QUARTER, JERUSALEM, END OF 19TH CENTURY. FIRST COOPERATIVE HOUSING PROJECT.
IN PALESTINE.

155. MINARET, END OF 19TH CENTURY, SAFED. ▶

156. BARSKY.
HERZLIYA SECONDARY SCHOOL, JAFFA-TEL-AVIV, 1906.

157. ALEX BERWALD. HAIFA TECHNICAL COLLEGE, 1914. ▼

158. RICHARD KAUFMANN. PLAN FOR A SYNAGOGUE IN REHAVIA,
JERUSALEM, (NOT IMPLEMENTED).

▼   159.   COURT OF "HURVA" SYNAGOGUE,
OLD CITY OF JERUSALEM. 18TH CENTURY.

160. CLIFFORD HOLIDAY. BIBLE SOCIETY BUILDING, JERUSALEM, 1930.

161. CLIFFORD HOLIDAY. SCOTTISH CHURCH, JERUSALEM, 1930.

162.   YOHANAN RATNER. BUILDINGS OF JEWISH NATIONAL FUND AND JEWISH FOUNDATION, JERUSALEM, 1930.

163.   LEOPOLD KRAKAUER. DINNING HALL, TEL-YOSEF COLLECTIVE SETTLEMENT, 1931.   ▶

164. ERICH MENDELSOHN. ISRAEL NATIONAL BANK (FORMERLY: ANGLO-PALESTINE BANK), JERUSALEM, 1937

165. ERICH MENDELSOHN. MT. SCOPUS MEDICAL CENTER, JERUSALEM, 1937. ▶

166. ERICH MENDELSOHN. MT. SCOPUS MEDICAL CENTER, JERUSALEM, 1937.

167. ARYEH SHARON; BENJAMIN IDELSON. BEERSHEBA HOSPITAL, 1956. ▶

168. ROBERT BANNET. SHOPPING CENTER, RAMAT-AVIV, 1960.

169. S. AND M. NADLER. RUPIN INSTITUTION, EMEK HEFER, 1948. ▶

170. DOV CARMI. HISTADRUT (LABOR FEDERATION) HEADQUARTERS, TEL-AVIV, 1955.

171.   DOV CARMI AND ZEEV RECHTER. MANN AUDITORIUM TEL-AVIV, 1959. FRONT VIEW.

172.   DOV CARMI AND ZEEV RECHTER. MANN AUDITORIUM TEL-AVIV 1959. INTERIOR.

173. ARYEH SHARON; BENJAMIN IDELSON. WORKERS' BANK, TEL-AVIV, 1961.

175. JOSEPH NEUFELD. HADASSAH MEDICAL CENTER, EIN KEREM, JERUSALEM ▶

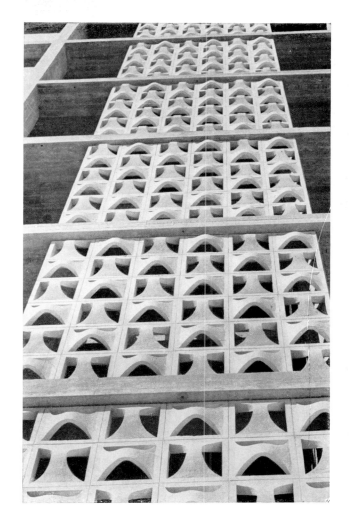

174. JOSEPH NEUFELD. HADASSAH MEDICAL CENTER,
EIN KEREM, JERUSALEM, 1961. CONCRETE FRETWORK, DETAIL.

176. ARYEH ELHANANI;
ARYEH SHARON;
BENJAMIN IDELSON.
YAD VASHEM
MEMORIAL SHRINE,
JERUSALEM, INTERIOR.

177. ARYEH ELHANANI;
ARYEH SHARON;
BENJAMIN IDELSON.
YAD VASHEM
MEMORIAL SHRINE,
JERUSALEM.

178. JOSEPH NEUFELD, ARCHITECT;
MARC CHAGALL. PAINTER:
STAINED GLASS WINDOWS,
HADASSAH MEDICAL CENTER,
EIN KEREM, JERUSALEM, 1961.

179. JOSEPH NEUFELD.
SYNAGOGUE
HADASSAH MEDICAL CENTER,
EIN KEREM, JERUSALEM, 1961.

181. S. AND M. NADLER; S. POZNER; HANAN EVRON; ZIVA ARMONI; ABRAHAM YASKY;
      A. ALEKSANDRONI. NATIONAL LIBRARY, HEBREW UNIVERSITY, 1961.

◀   180.   DOV CARMI; S. MELTZER. ORT VOCATIONAL SCHOOL, TEL-AVIV, 1958, COURT.

182. RECHTER; ZARHI; RECHTER. REST HOME, NAZARETH

183. K. AND R. FELDMAN. MOSLEM ORPHANAGE, ACRE.

184. NAHUM ZOLOTOV. HOSTEL, AVDAT.

185. A. SHARON; B. IDELSON. CHURCHILL ASSEMBLY HALL, TECHNION CAMPUS, HAIFA, 1958.

187.   Y. SHALGI AND A. ROBINSON. GYMNASIUM, KEFAR HA-MAKKABIYA. COURT.

◄   186.   ROBERT BANNET. BRODETSKY HOUSE, RAMAT-AVIV, 1957.

188. 189. 190. HOUSING PROJECTS IN TEL-AVIV AND HAIFA.

191.   A. YASKY AND A. ALEKSANDRONI. APARTMENT HOUSE, TEL-AVIV, 1961.

192.   A. SHARON; B. IDELSON. ONE-STORY HOUSING, NAZARETH.

193.   ROBERT BANNET. RAMAT-AVIV HOUSING PROJECTS, 1962.

194.   A. YASKY AND A. ALEKSANDRONI. APARTMENT HOUSE, BEERSHEBA, 1962.

195.   VITKOVER AND BAUMANN. HOTEL SHERATON, TEL-AVIV, 1961.

196.   Y. YASHAR; D. EYTAN. APARTMENT HOUSE, JAFFA.

197.   SHEMUEL MESTIECHKIN. CHICKEN HOUSE, COLLECTIVE SETTLEMENT, 1955.

198. ARYEH ELHANANI. WIXS HOUSE, WEIZMANN INSTITUTE, REHOVOT. PATIO.

199. D. A. BRUTZKUS. APPLIED PHYSICS' LABORATORIES, HEBREW UNIVERSITY CAMPUS, JERUSALEM, 1958.

200. ROBERT BANNET. DINNING HALL, GIVAT-BRENNER COLLECTIVE SETTLEMENT, 1962.

◀ 201. NAHUM ZOLOTOV. BUILDING, TEL-AVIV, 1959.

202. CARMI; MELTZER; CARMI. ORT VOCATIONAL SCHOOL, TEL-AVIV, 1958. PORCH.

203.   S. GILAD; D. KHAVKIN. APARTMENT HOUSE, RAMAT-HADAR, HAIFA.

204.   M. WEINROB; A. MANSFELD. HYDRAULIC LABORATORY, TECHNION, HAIFA, 1957.

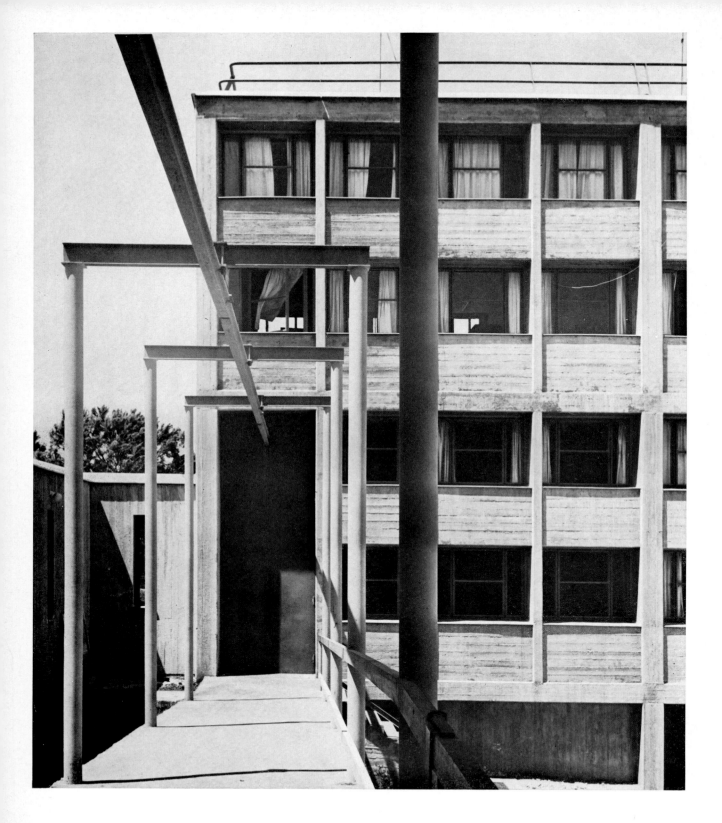

206. A. HASHIMSHONI. VOCATIONAL SCHOOL, TECHNION, HAIFA, 1959.

207. CARMI; MELTZER; CARMI.
EL-AL BUILDING TEL-AVIV, 1963.

◄ 208. CARMI; MELTZER; CARMI.
EL-AL BUILDING, TEL-AVIV, 1963

209. A. YASKY; A. ALEKSANDRONI. CENTRAL MARKET, BEERSHEBA, 1962. VENDOR'S STAND.

210. HEINZ RAU. HEBREW UNION COLLEGE JERUSALEM 1962.

211. S. MESTIECHKIN. NAUTICAL SCHOOL, CAESAREA, 1947.

212. Y. VITKOVER; A. BAUMANN. GLASS MUSEUM, TEL-AVIV, FRONT FACED WITH PORCELAIN, 1959.

214. ABBA ELHANANI. PHILIP MURRAY HOUSE, EILAT, 1958.

◀ 213. CARMI; MELTZER; CARMI. WISE AUDITORIUM, HEBREW UNIVERSITY, JERUSALEM, 1957. INTERIOR.

215. ABBA ELHANANI. PHILIP MURRAY HOUSE, EILAT, 1958. INTERIOR.

216. HEBREW UNIVERSITY CAMPUS JERUSALEM, 1962. VIEW FROM NORTHEAST.

217. HEBREW UNIVERSITY CAMPUS JERUSALEM, 1962 GENERAL VIEW. ▶

218. RECHTER; ZARHI; RECHTER. DEPARTMENT OF ARCHEOLOGY, HEBREW UNIVERSITY CAMPUS, JERUSALEM, 1960.

220. CARMI; MELTZER; CARMI. HEBREW UNIVERSITY CAMPUS, JERUSALEM, 1958. ADMINISTRATION BUILDING. ▶

219. D. A. BRUTZKUS. BOTANICAL LABORATORIES, HEBREW UNIVERSITY CAMPUS, JERUSALEM, 1955.

222.   A. YASKY; S. POZNER. COURT, KAPLAN BUILDING, HEBREW UNIVERSITY CAMPUS, JERUSALEM, 1958.   ▶

221.   CARMI; MELTZER; CARMI. WISE BUILDING, HEBREW UNIVERSITY CAMPUS, JERUSALEM, 1957

223.   YOHANAN RATNER. PEVSNER HALL, BIRAM BUILDING, REALI HIGH SCHOOL, HAIFA, 1962.

224.   S. MESTIECHKIN. THEATER, HEBREW UNIVERSITY CAMPUS, JERUSALEM, 1958.   ▶

225.   HEINZ RAU; D. REZNIK, SYNAGOGUE, HEBREW UNIVERSITY CAMPUS, JERUSALEM, 1957.

CRAFTS

JOHN CHENEY

DESIGN &

FIVE: CRAFTS AND DESIGN by JOHN CHENEY

The land of Israel shares the ancient beginnings of civilization with the Middle East in general. In the earliest times it lay across both the land and sea routes of the two great civilizations of Egypt and Mesopotamia, and must early have been exposed to both cultures.

Archaeological excavations throughout the country are constantly turning up new facts regarding the history and pre-history of the area, yet the journey into the past is still far from complete.

Archaeology depends largely on handicraft remains, especially the styles of pottery, for the dating and cultural identification of peoples. Israel provides may examples of objects at once utilitarian and aesthetically satisfying.

It has long been believed that the first glass production in the world by the Phoenicians occurred on the coast north of Haifa, and certainly many beautiful specimens of glass are to be seen in the country's museums. On the nearby Carmel Mountains, a much earlier paleolithic culture fashioned tools, knives, arrows and spearheads from the flints now popularly known as *Elijah's melons*. Some areas are still literally covered with broken or half-finished works.

Man here, as everywhere else, identified himself as a tool- and weapon-maker. He was, consequently, both designer and craftsman.

The "Habiru", mentioned in early writings in Babylonia (c. 2600 B.C.), in Egypt (c. 2000 B.C.) and Palestine and Syria (c. 1400 B.C.) as invaders of the cultivated lands from the deserts of the area generally known now as Arabia, may or may not be accepted as the forefathers of the Biblical Hebrews. However, it is a fact that Abraham and his children were patriarchal nomadic herdsmen living in semi-arid areas and in the classic pattern, encroaching on the more developed agricultural settlements under pressure of population increase or natural disasters such as drought in the home pastures.

An interesting circumstance is that in Israel, even in this year 1965, one can still get a good idea of this distant past through the lives of the living Bedouins. Despite cars and canned foods, they maintain almost unchanged the patriarchal nomadic herding economy and ecology of five thousand years ago.

Until permanently settled, they also maintain many of the primitive handicrafts of the third millennium B.C. Cloth manufacured in a factory in Tel Aviv is made into the beautiful voluminous robes of a past era, still best suited to the heat and cold of the desert.

The history of the land of Israel is a history of conquest and re-conquest, Egyptians, Hittites and Hyksos, Babylonians, Greeks, Persians, Romans, Crusaders, Arabs, Turks and the English, in turn overran the country. Each of these, as well as the Jews themselves in their various returns to the land, has left its relics in stone, clay and metal, which constitute a bewilderingly rich heritage of civilizations and of styles in crafts and arts.

Craftsmen, particularly weavers, familiar with the patterns and colour combinations of folk costumes, have come to Israel from all parts of Europe. A rich variety of materials has therefore been woven on hand looms. From 1955 to 1960 dirndl skirts of these materials became almost a national costume for girls and young women. More sophisticated styles were also developed, but the fashion has now largely passed, to be replaced, perhaps unfortunately, by blue jeans and skin-tight pants.

Another European folk art which has been developed in Israel is that of burning and tooling designs on wood and leather.

The local Arab, Bedouin and Druze artifacts are a great source of inspiration to Israeli craftsmen.

ANCIENT INFLUENCES. 1700-400 B.C.E.

226. EARTHENWARE JUG,
LATE BRONZE AGE 1600–1500 B.C.E.

227. HYKSOS JARS, 1800–1700 B.C.E.

228. AMPHORA, 5TH CENTURY B.C.E.

229. ARYBALLOS GLASS KNOWN AS
"PHOENICIAN" 500–400 B.C.E.

230. ALABASTRON, GLASS KNOWN AS
"PHOENICIAN" 500–400 B.C.E.

231. TEL-AVIV, 1934.

232. TEL-AVIV, 1963.

The Arabs, the Druze and the Yemenites produced a type of sewn basket of plaited straw, stitched with brightly coloured raffia. The best of these are very beautiful, but their usefulness is limited by the essential weakness of the material. Serious study is now in progress to make them of more durable stuffs.

A much more subtly beautiful basket is made by the Bedouin. Of rather coarse straw, it is woven, very flexible, and usually of shopping-basket size. Such baskets are very strong and tightly woven, and have seen many years of use for carrying earth and stone on building sites, and as panniers for the ubiquitous donkey.

Arab pottery in this country is almost all of a coarse, soft, low-fired clay which is porous. The shapes are traditional, some recent pieces being almost indistinguishable from pots made three and four thousand years ago. This art is rapidly being supplanted by badly-conceived "modern" forms, and hand-painted (with paint, of course, not with glazes) decoration.

Arab copper and brassware, once nearly the equal to that of Damascus, have been cheapened by the demands of the souvenir trade, and have almost entirely disappeared.

Of all the immigrant groups, the Yemenites are probably alone in bringing into Israel a complete, unadulterated and long-established folk tradition with all its arts and crafts. The story of their mass exodus from the Yemen and their return to the Promised Land, on foot, by sea, and aboard a "flying carpet", is well-known. They left the sixth century A.D., and arrived in the twentieth, with no intermediate stages.

Consequently, Yemenite silver filigree, embroidery, copperware, brassware, and fabrics, have made a massive impact on crafts in Israel. Rather unwilling to accept styles of the neighbouring Arabs, the Israeli is delighted to learn from the example of Yemenite Jews. Although there are, of course, strong resemblances between their work and that of the Arabs, the Yemenite Jewish crafts are distinguished by a refinement, and by a special ethnic and religious character. Inevitably, in adapting these articles to souvenir production, there has been some loss of quality, and some bizarre errors of taste have been committed. Nevertheless, Yemenite work has become one of the basic ingredients in the slowly developing Israeli craft style.

Of the native arts of neighbouring Persia, the only one which has at all affected Israeli craftsmanship has been rug weaving. Although many Persian Jews have now settled in Israel, it would seem they had not been craftsmen in their native country. If they were at all familiar with Persian crafts it was rather as merchants than as makers.

Both public and private looms have attempted to weave Persian-style carpets here in Israel, but these efforts have proved abortive, since the tremendous amount of hand labour and the time involved are not consonant with the economy of a modern state. It can be assumed, however, that the memory of the fine handicrafts of Persia must have left some Israeli craftsmen with an image which will one day serve as source material for the development of crafts in this country.

Like the Persian, the immigration of North African Jews had little influence on the craft situation. A number of rug makers from Morocco have continued to work at their old trade, but the introduction of finer and softer yarns produced on a commercial basis, in the place of the hand-spun sheep and goat wool yarns primitively dyed, has resulted in a product both less durable and less distinctive. Again, the economics of an advanced state with complex labour legislation has made such work disproportionately expensive.

The cast silver, and ornaments, buckles, belts and so on of North Africa appear only as heirlooms brought in by the immigrants. I know of no local production of such work, which has a distinctive style and beauty quite different from that of filigree.

In the 1930s, though some came earlier, a substantial group of craftsmen came from Europe to settle in Israel. They came for the most part from Western Europe, and especially from Germany, Austria, Czechoslovakia and France. They brought with them highly developed skills, having been trained in the best craft schools, and possessed of a knowledge of contemporary thought and philosophy in the fields of craft and design.

Most of this group settled at first in Jerusalem but now they are scattered about the country. Several of them, for example, Keiner, Wolpert and Gumbel, became teachers at Bezalel. These were largely responsible for the training of a new generation of native born or young immigrant Israelis, some of whom are now themselves teaching. This continuity has established a school of relatively modern European design in contrast to the earlier group which advocated the adoption and modernisation of local contemporary as well as ancient Middle Eastern crafts.

An unfortunate effect has been the production of inferior abstractions based on baroque originals. A fortunate one has been the stimulation of a widespread controversy among both craftsmen and people in general as to what is or should be true Israeli style. Apart from a few isolated examples, however, such a style has not yet appeared.

Most of the more acceptable craft designs have been produced by individuals strongly imbued with a feeling for the new state of Israel and for its past. However, there are now some Israeli designers who have remained *au fait* with developments in international design, and who have, indeed, made their own special contribution to it.

In general the younger generation of craftsman in Israel consists of graduates of the Bezalel school. To understand them, it is necessary to know what the school has taught or attempted to teach. In the beginning it was regarded mainly as a means of fostering an indigenous new art in the Jewish community in Palestine. Even at the turn of the century, the craft emphasis was on imitation of older craft objects of the European diaspora, or on the imitation of Middle Eastern peasant artifacts. A very high standard of workmanship and finish was requaired, and training was on the old European basis of a long apprenticeship and the subjection of the ideas and the creative urge of the apprentice to the dictates of the master. This system produced competent workers in several branches, but chiefly, under the direction of Schatz and, later, Ardon, in the fine arts, especially painting. Some of Israel's best painters made their start at Bezalel.

We have already written of the influx of Western European craftsmen in the 1930s. Under their tuition, the old perfectionism was generally maintained, though style leaped forward by a whole generation in a few years, and the interest in local and strictly Jewish art forms partly disappeared.

During the past decade the school has deteriorated both economically and educationally. This situation seems to arise less from a lack of competent instructors than from a lack of proper direction. No one has been exactly sure what the school should teach to prepare students for work in a growing, changing country. One tendency seems to have been to make Bezalel a finishing school for well-to-do young ladies and gentlemen who do not intend to enter the liberal professions, and do not need to seek employment to survive. If this seems harsh, let it be said that the same affliction has troubled the best art schools in the United States for half a century, and, one suspects, for even longer in Europe.

Another negative factor has been the almost complete lack of co-operation and co-ordination between Bezalel-trained craftsmen and the country's craft industries. The school was originally planned to provide trained craftsmen either to work on their own account or in other people's small workshops. Contrary to that expectation, Israel has developed a kind of semi-mass-production factory craft industry where their skills are little wanted and their artistic talents mistrusted.

As a result, Israel can today boast of first-rate craftsmen capable of holding their own internationally in such fields as silver metalwork, jewellery, weaving, textile printing and ceramics. Yet at the same time ninety per cent of the craft wares we export are in the worst taste.

Recently the government has revived its interest in the school. A new director, the architect Darnel, has been entrusted with the task, which I believe he has the ability to carry out, of integrating Bezalel and its students into the artistic and economic life of present-day Israel.

As in the other crafts, the best hand-potters in Israel are good by international standards, although their talents have only just begun to affect Israeli ceramics.

Among the older potters mention should be made of Hedwig Grossman, Hannah Zunz-Harag and Cahana, all of whom trained in Europe. The three present an interesting cross-section of styles. From the beginning Grossman adopted local clays and typical Near Eastern forms for her creations which feature slip decoration in simple patterns and in earth colours. Harag's work is classical in style, depending chiefly on perfection of form. She has made a serious effort to revive the art of terra sigillata which flourished in the Eastern Mediterranean in Roman times. Cahana has always been to the forefront of experiment in ceramic form and decoration, studying Pre-Columbian, African and Oriental styles, and applying Cubist principles to his pots. At the same time, he succeeds in preserving the useful qualities of the vessels he makes.

Among the younger artists, Nehemiah Azaz has been able to apply his talents to industrial production through his years as designer for the Harsa factory. Although he considers himself basically a sculptor rather than a potter, and despite the fact that many of his vases are more sculpture than utensil, he will perhaps forgive me for saying that his useful wares, such as his coffee sets, are among his best work.

Elspeth Cohen, designer for the Lapid factory, has also been responsible for some of the best Israeli ceramics. Her style is clean, austere, and classical, and in some ways reminiscent of contemporary Scandinavian design. It is unfortunate that Lapid is not equipped to produce large tableware, since her talent is admirably suited to this field.

It is interesting to compare two other young potters, since they reflect the influence of their teachers, as well as each having her own peculiar talents and individual response to her surroundings. Gedulla Schweig, one of Grossman's pupils, has retained her teacher's interest in local forms and earth colours, but being a native-born Israeli, she has felt the dynamic spirit of her generation. Her work, therefore, though far less fine than her teacher's, is distinguished by its greater size and boldness of conception, and there is a charming gaiety in her animal forms.

Jean Meyer, a pupil of Harag, was not born in Israel, although she has lived most of her adult life in the collective settlement of Ein Ha-Shofet. Though she still aspires to her teacher's perfection of form her pots become more vital and earthy as her own style matures.

Two other young women, Yehudit Meyer and Yokheved Marx, working in Beersheba, have been making attractively decorated pottery. This development will lead to a wider range of design, and the production of more durable and useful craftware.

Other potters worth mentioning include Penina Harel of Jerusalem, who fashions figurines in a distinctive style combining archaeological designs and contemporary abstraction, and Shelli Harari of Tel Aviv, who makes large pitchers in bird and animal forms. Her glazes are varied and subtle.

There is a growing local market for fine hand-thrown ceramics, as well as for a substantial quantity sold to tourists. However, the difficulty and cost of shipping have so far seriously limited the export of this ware. It is to be hoped that in the near future closer coöperation between individual craftsmen and local factories will make possible the export of this excellent ware in appreciable quantities.

In the last few years, an interest in architectural ceramics has developed. The groundwork for this was laid in the artists' village at Ein Hod, where several members of the group, including Bezalel Schatz, Yitzhak Mambush, Aviva Margalit, Shealtiel, Shulamit Tal and Aryeh Korn are very active.

Cahana executed some of the first ceramic murals, among the most successful of which were those in the Haifa Underground, and those in the ocean liner the *S. S. Herzl*. Bezalel Schatz's murals at Abu Gosh and at the Desert Inn at Beersheba are also interesting, as is Gedulla Schweig's recent mural for a bank in Jerusalem.

The production of porcelain at the Naaman factory and of semi-vitreous ware at Palceramic, Lapid and Harsa in recent years has stimulated a general improvement in the design of commercial tableware, so, that it seems reasonable to hope that an international standard may be achieved in this field within the next few years.

The glass industry in Israel was until very recently strictly utilitarian. Sheet and safety glass are made by Phoenicia in Haifa, and bottles and similar containers by Phoenicia and Gavish in Rishon Le-Zion and by Tsor in Bat Yam. Technical and scientific glass of good quality is being made by Phoenikia of Jerusalem and several smaller workshops.

It was impossible, however, to obtain decent drinking glasses in Israel until a year or two ago, and anything that could have been called "art" glass did not exist.

The present activity in glass production was initiated by the installation at Gavish of a new furnace for barium and lead-crystal glass, and the training of a team of glass blowers. The product is of good quality and of current European style.

At about the same time, Tsor began to produce what is locally known as Hebron glass because of its resemblance to the ware made in that ancient city, now in Jordan. This coloured rather crude glass, studded with bubbles, lends itself remarkably well to ancient forms.

The new Shafrir factory has begun to make a handworked glass similar to the Murano glass of Italy. Designed by Nehemiah Azaz, its best products are of fine quality, and have a character all their own.

A different kind of glassware, fashioned by craftsmen from glass tubing by means of oxyacetylene heat, has appeared in the shops of recent years. The technique which is based on the glass-blower's skills, was devised originally for industrial use. The pioneer in this new craft is Bar-Tal of Haifa, who, at his best, works his material like a true artist. Several younger men, including Necker of Jerusalem, Anshel and Arbel of Haifa, and Rika of Tel Aviv, are progressing rapidly in this art. The unique features of this work are its resemblance to the ancient forms of Phoenicia, Rome and Greece; and its fairly successful reproduction of the patina of the glass of antiquity. In the field of silverware and jewellery there are so many competent and talented craftsmen that it is impossible to discuss each one. This being so, a few will have to represent them all.

Of the oldest generation of Israeli silverworkers, Gumbel of Jerusalem and Yohanan Peter of Ein Hod are European-trained men of substantial talent. Gumbel and Berman of Jerusalem recently won two out of the five major prizes in the International Silver Company World competition for sterling silver flatware designs, against some of the best European, American and Scandinavian designers.

Peter's jewellery is on display in many European museums, and Kurt Fefferman of Haifa was recently awarded a gold medal for jewellery design at the *Sonderschau* in Munich.

Although the two younger men, Berman and Fefferman were trained in Israel, all four are craftsmen in the European tradition and are modern and international in outlook in the best sense of those terms. Peter perhaps most shows the influence of his Israeli environment particularly in his interesting use of local non-precious stones and ceramics in conjunction with silver.

Workers in copper and brass in Israel range from the most sophisticated to the ultimate in banality. Perhaps the best work of all has been that of the Iraqi immigrant Avraham Haddad, who has recently spent much time in

Paris. His education in the philosophy of modern art has not eradicated his oriental heritage.

Much credit must be given to the Yaad group consisting of Bezalel, Louise, and Zahara Schatz and Jean David, whose experiments with raised and incised decorations on metal and in combining various materials, have established a trend, which, for better or worse, has come to be recognised as typical of Israeli craftsmanship. Berman and his Taas company, Yitzhak Bir, Kurt Fefferman, Mordechai Blum, Yehiel Hadami and others have also produced very creditable work in similar materials.

Despite all this talent, however, the copper and brassware market of Israel is still being flooded with lop-sided, badly-coloured and unfinished products by the local factories.

Artistic enamels have not been much developed in Israel. Some original work in this line has been produced by Jean David, but his wide interest in painting and commercial art have prevented him from developing this talent to the full. Ilana Hareli of Ramatayim is the most consistent producer of first class enamelwork. The technical skill of Madame Schwadron of Haifa is also outstanding. She has a fine sense of colour, and her multiple firings produce truly jewel-like effects.

Handwoven textiles in Israel are largely the work of a group of West European craftsmen who immigrated to Jerusalem in the 1930. Their acknowledged leader is Julia Keiner who taught textile weaving at Bezalel until a year ago. Her students include most of the active younger weavers in the country: and she herself has received recognition internationally for the design and quality of her weaving, especially for the great curtain for the United Nations building.

Capable weavers in the European tradition include Hanna Barkai, Ruth Lavie, Miriam Kadish and others. One of the most talented younger weavers and teachers is Neora Warshavsky, at present weaver-in-charge for the Maskit organisation. She has achieved an interesting synthesis of European and local oriental techniques and patterns.

Two commercial manufacturers, Horn of Eytun and Karshi of Migdal Ha-Emek have also made substantial contributions to quality and design in their chosen field.

Only in the past few years have original prints become a factor in the cotton textile market. This season (1965) between five and ten per cent of the printed cottons made in Israel are of local design. Since the industry must now compete in international export markets, local design is acquiring greater importance.

The revival of textile printing in Israel may be credited to a small group of artists which includes Erika Meiselmann-Kluger, Baruch Urwand, Jean David, Avraham Levine and Naomi Levine. The prints on display at the international fashion show held in conjunciton with the State of Israel Bond Drive of 1958–59, and in which many top Paris *couturiers* participated, were so successful that local producers were encouraged to employ Israeli designers for some of their new prints. Maskit especially is producing an unusually successful series.

Aware of the export potential, the government has just opened a studio for textile printing under designer Goldstein who received his training in Paris.

Outstanding as a batik printer is Shulamit Levenstein of Kiryat Tivon. Though entirely self-taught she has a marvellous feeling for pattern and colour, and her technique for both silk and cotton is of a high standard.

Israel has classic examples of historical mosaic (see, for example, the UNESCO publication of the mosaics of the Bet Alpha Synagogue). Specimens from the Roman and Byzantine eras have been discovered at Caesarea, Tabgha and elsewhere in a fine state of preservation. Carmel and Galilee yellow limestone was the common material for gold backgrounds to mosaics of the entire Mediterranean region during the Byzantine period.

Naturally, therefore, a number of craftsmen has been attracted by this art, and good work has been accomplished in the form of wall tablets, plaques and smaller pieces. The most talented Israeli mosaicists are David Palombo and Naomi Hendrichs of Jerusalem, and Miriam and Mordechai Gumbel of Tivon. Palombo's creative imagination and love of experiment have produced some extremely interesting works of art.

Several attempts have been made to manufacture mosaics for the general market. The most successful to date has been that of the workshop at Kibbutz Eilon, where the new technique of setting the tesserae in polyester plaster instead of cement produces much lighter and stronger panels suitable for both interior and exterior decoration.

Israel has had considerable success in the international fashion world in several lines, notably in Maskit's desert coats designed by Fini Leitersdorf; Yemenite embroidery for evening gowns; bathing suits by Gottex, Diva and Elemko; knitwear jersey of Aled, Jercoli and Elanit; and poplin rainwear by Salpeter and Gutfreund. There is reason to suppose that this branch of Israeli design will grow steadily, especially since fashion is by its nature always open to innovation and the original approach.

Fine woodwork in Israel has always been limited by the scarcity of the basic material, the only fine woods available in quantity locally being olive and lemon, although recently experiments have been made with eucalyptus wood. Standard furniture woods are European boxwood, and a soft mahogany imported from Africa, gabun. A new import, afrormosia, a type of teak, has added to the material available.

Despite this problem, a small group of craftsmen is producing fine woodwork. Rudy Lehman, now of Givatayim, but originally of the Jerusalem craft group, has produced monumental sculpture as well as beautiful miniatures in wood. His most charming pieces are animal figures. Aharon Bezalel, a former student of Lehman, now teaching at the Seligsburg Crafts School in Jerusalem, carves fine miniatures frequently based on archaeological specimens. Ruth Sternschuss-Tsarfati tends more towards abstraction, combining a sensitive taste with a flair for form and proportion. S. V. Loebl of Safed is another of the original Jerusalem group now producing wooden bowls, plates, and tableware of beautiful design and execution.

Even if doll-making is not ordinarily considered an art, one local dollmaker must be regarded as a true artist. Edith Samuel of Rishon Le-Zion has, with her stylised costume dolls, produced charming works of art which can serve as reminders of the diverse types of Jews coming to Israel from all over the world. Copies of these and similar types of dolls have been made, but none can compare even remotely with Miss Samuel's originals.

233.   WOODEN CAKE MOLDS, LEBANON.

235. SPICE BOX, SILVER, PARTLY GILDED
EARLY 18TH CENTURY GERMANY. "BEZALEL," JERUSALEM.

◀ 234. HANUKKA LAMP, BRASS, 18TH CENTURY, MOROCCO.
HANUKKA LAMP, GOLD AND SILVER, 18TH CENTURY, GALICIA;
HANUKKA LAMP, BRASS CASTING 19TH CENTURY MOROCCO.

236. HANUKKA LAMP, SILVER FILIGREE,
18TH CENTURY, THE UKRAINE, "BEZALEL" JERUSALEM.

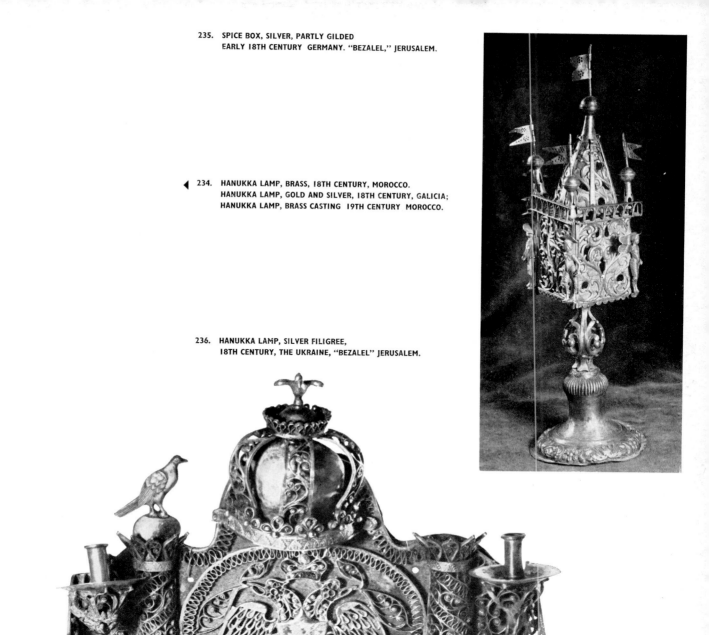

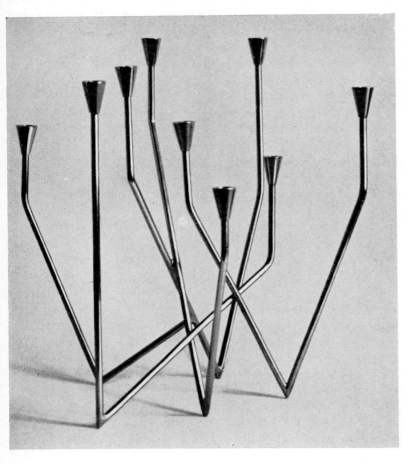

237. KURT FEFFERMAN. HANUKKA LAMP, BRONZE.

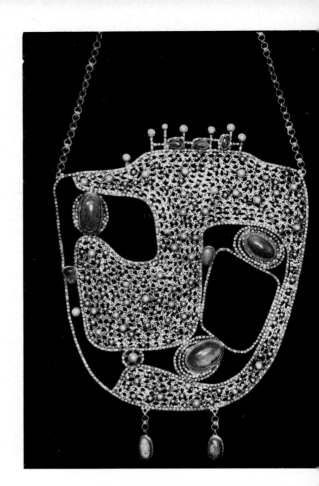

238. ERIKA MEISELMANN-KLUGER. TORAH-SCROLL DECORA

241. BLACK EARTHENWARE JUG, GAZA, EARLY 20TH CENTURY.

239. DAVID GUMBEL. TORAH-SCROLL CROWN.

240. TORAH-SCROLL CROWN AND "POMEGRANATES" (OVOID ORNAMENTS) SILVER, 18TH CENTURY, ITALY. "BEZALEL" JERUSALEM.

242. COFFEE MORTAR (JORON), BEDOUIN, NEGEV.

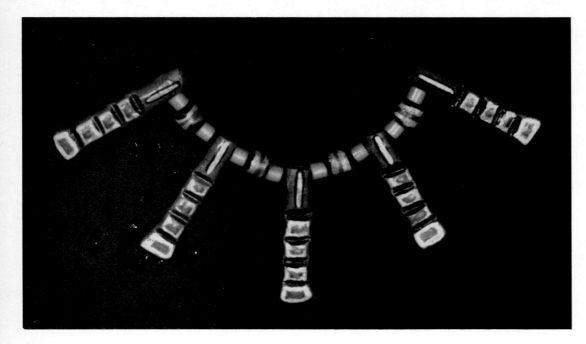

243. SHULAMIT TAL. NECKLACE, CERAMIC.

244. YITZHAK DAR. NECKLACE, SILVER.

245. YOHANAN PETER. BROOCH, COPPER AND ENAMEL.

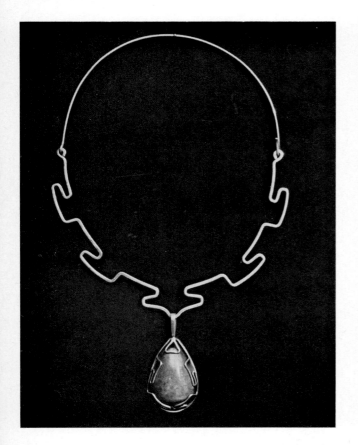

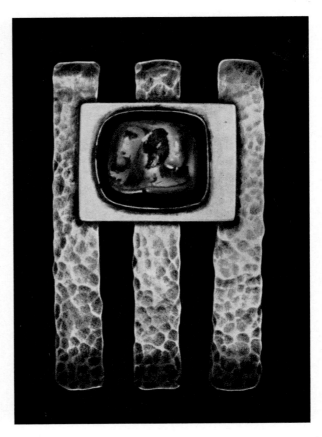

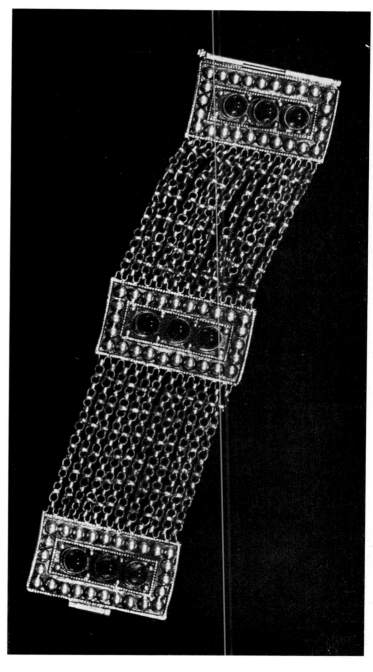

246. SILVER BRACELET, YEMENITE HANDIWORK, WIZO.

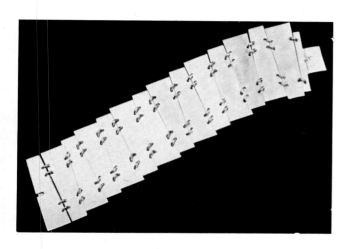

247. HAYIM PAZ. BRACELET SILVER.

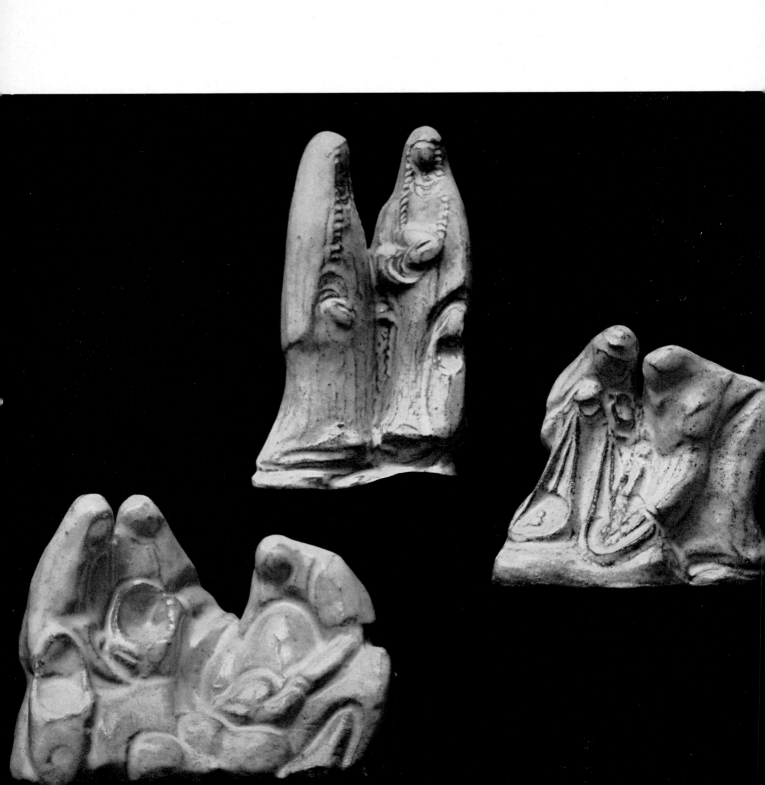

249. HAVA SAMUEL. PLATE AND JUG, CERAMIC.

◀ 248. HAVA SAMUEL. WOMEN IN THE MARKET PALCE, CERAMIC.

250. HEDWIG GROSSMAN. ASSORTED CERAMIC VESSELS.

251. HANNAH HARAG. THREE JUGS, CERAMIC.

252. HEDWIG GROSSMAN. TWO JUGS, CERAMIC.

253. GLASS JUGS, MANUFACTURED BY "BAT-SHEVA".

254. GEDULLA SCHWEIG. SHEEP, CERAMIC.

255. GEDULLA SCHWEIG. CERAMIC.

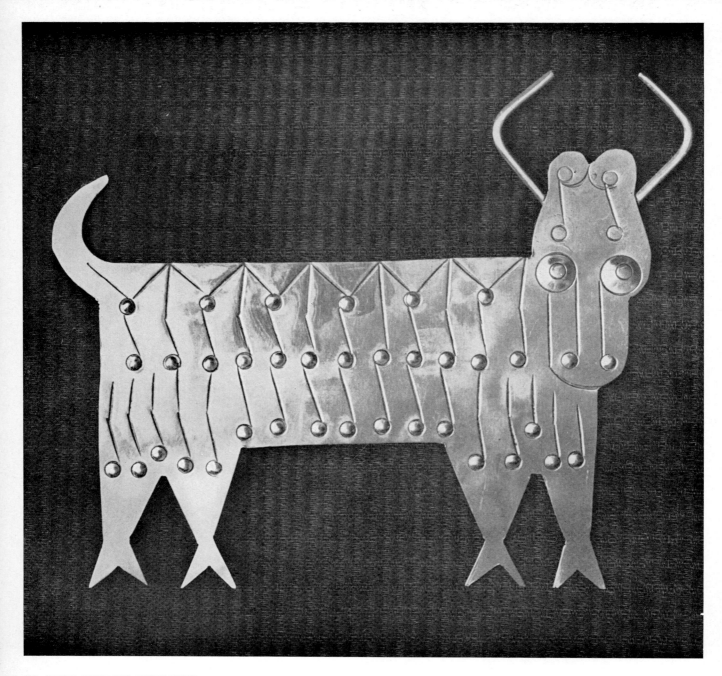

256. BEZALEL SCHATZ. BULL, BEATEN COPPER.

257. ARYEH KORN. VENICE, CERAMIC RELIEF.

258. SHULAMIT TAL. CERAMIC RELIEF.

259. DOLLS, MANUFACTURED BY WIZO.

260. PENINA HAREL. CERAMIC FIGURES.

261. YEMENITE BRIDE IN ALL HER FINERY.

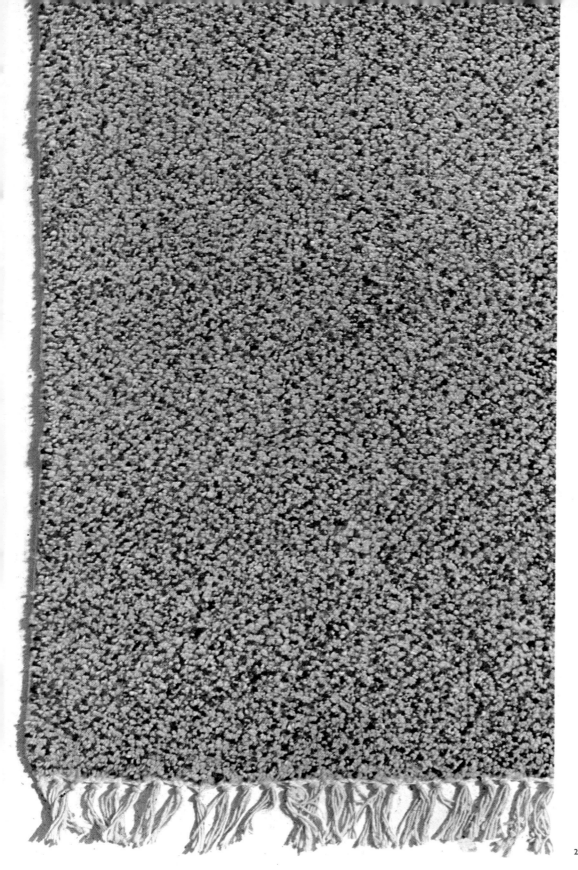

262. JULIA KEINER. WOOL RUG.

263. ZAHARA SCHATZ. PAINTING WITH PRESSWAX AND WIRE.

264. SHELLI HARARI. CERAMICWARE.

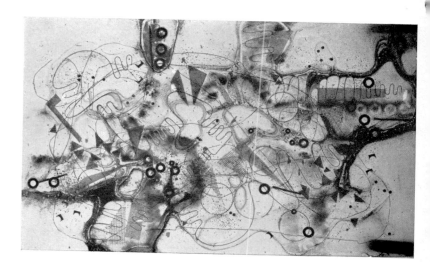

265. ZAHARA SCHATZ. PAINTING WITH PRESSWAX AND WIRES.

266.   ELSPETH COHEN. COFFEE SET, CERAMIC.

267.   JEAN MEYER. BOWL AND BOTTLE, CERAMIC.

268.   YEHUDIT MEYER AND YOKHEVED MAR.

R AND BOTTLE, CERAMIC.

269. ELSPETH COHEN. CUP AND BOTTLE, CERAMIC.

270. "PALCERAMIC" CASSEROLE. MANUFACTURED PORCELAIN PRODUCT.

271. "NAAMAN" JUG, MANUFACTURED PORCELAIN PRODUCT.

272. SHELLI HARARI. CERAMIC.

273. PENINA HAREL. FIGURES, CERAMIC.

274. DAVID GUMBEL. TEA SET,
SILVER AND WALNUT.

276. DAVID GUMBEL. CUTLERY, SILVER. ▶

275. DAVID GUMBEL. COFFEE SET,
SILVER AND WALNUT.

277. "HAYADIT," PARDES-HANNAH, OLIVE-WOOD TABLE UTENSILS.

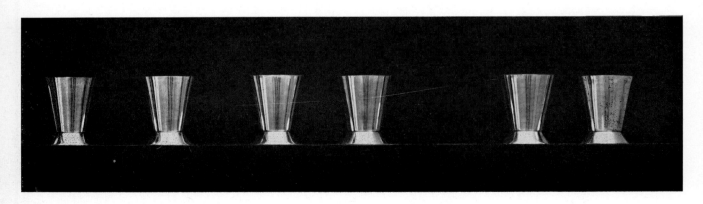

278. YITHAK BIR. SILVER WINE GLASSES.

279. PAPER STAND, HAZOREA COLLECTIVE SETTLEMENT.

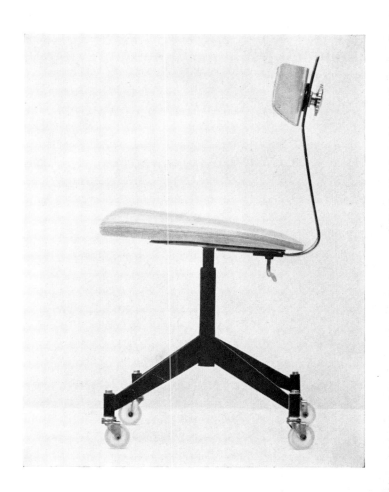

280. YITZHAK COHEN, "PALTECHNIKA": OFFICE CHAIR.

281. NEHEMIAH AZAZ. SCULPTURED WALL, HOTEL SHERATON, TEL-AVIV. (ARCHITECTS: VITKOVER-BAUMANN).

282–283. RUTH TSARFATI. WOODEN TOYS.

284. JEAN DAVID. POSTER.

285. JEAN DAVID. PLAYING CARD.

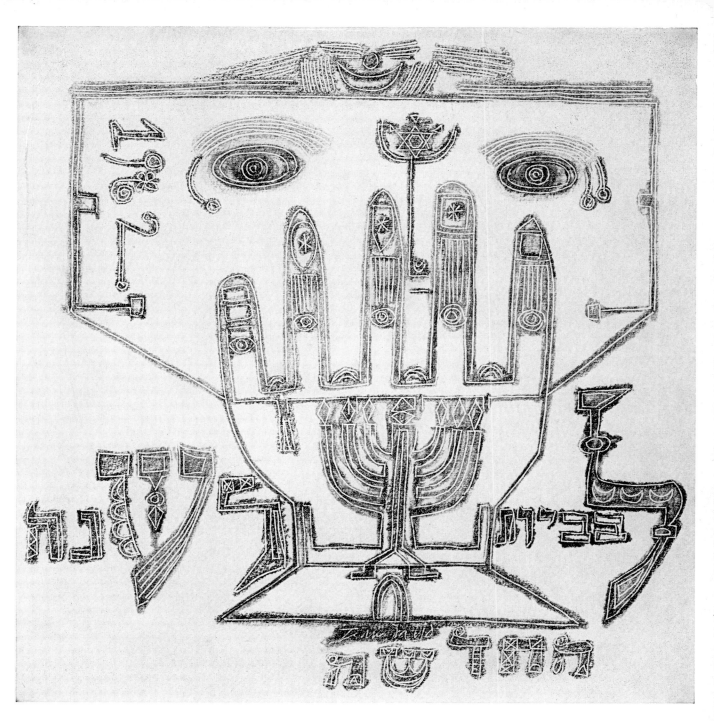

286. JEAN DAVID. NEW YEAR'S GREETING CARD.

287. EDITH SAMUEL.
BOYS, CLOTH DOLLS.

288. EDITH SAMUEL. THE ARTIST AS A CHILD,
CLOTH DOLL.

NAME INDEX *

Abramovitz 31
Agadati, Baruch 38
Agam, Yaacov 40, *94*
Alcalay, Aharon *28*
Alexandroni, A. *181, 191, 194, 209*
Angelico, Fra 5
Anshel 295
Arbel, 295
Ardon-Bronstein, Mordekhai 25, 26, 37,
    39, 291, *18, 19, 20, 21*
Argov, Michael 35, *92*
Arieli 31
Arikha, Avigdor 39, 40, *95, 96, 97, 98*
Armoni, Ziva *181*
Aroch, Arieh 42
Ascheim, Isidor 23, 24, *9*
Ashkenazi, Aharon 144
Atar 22
Avni, Shimon 28, 33, 43
Avniel 28, 35
Azaz, Nehemiah 293, 295, *281*

Bacon, Yehuda 38
Bamberger, Ruth 25
Bannet, Robert *168, 186, 193, 200*
Bar-el, Yoav 43
Barkai, Hannah 296
Bar-tal 295
Barsky *156*
Baser, Robert 144
Baumann, A. *195, 212, 281*
Behrens 218
Ben-Zvi, Ze'ev 143, 146, *114*
Bergner, Audrey 34, *48, 81*
Bergner, Yossl 36, 37, *27, 56, 57, 58*
Berlege 218
Berman 295, 296
Berwald, Alex 206, 207, 210, *157*
Bezalel, Aharon 298
Bezem, Naphtali 37, 38, *85*
Bir, Yitzhak 296, *278*
Blum, Mordechai 296

Boccioni, Umberto 140
Boneh, Schmuel 37, *60*
Bonnard, Pierre 29
Brancusi, Constantin 140, *106*
Braque, Georges 10
Brutzkus, D. A. *199, 219*
Budko 17
Buffet, Bernard 39

Cahana: see kahana, Aharon
Calder 140
Carmi, Dov 212, 213, *170, 171, 172, 180,
    202, 207, 208, 215, 220, 221*
Carmi (& Meltzer & Carmi) *180, 202,
    207, 208, 215, 220, 221* —
Castel, Moshe 22, 28, 30–33, *4*
Cezanne, Paul 18
Chagall, Marc 19, 37, *178*
Churchill, Sir Winston, Assembly Hall
    185
Cobra 41
Cohen, Elspeth 293, *266, 269*
Cohen, Yitzhak *280*
Constable, John 18

Dahan, Meir 143
Danziger, Yitzhak 144, 149, 150 *136–142*
Dar, Yitzhak *244*
Darnel 292
David, Jean 38, 296, 297, *76, 77, 284–286*
Dubuffet, Jean 41

Elhannani, Abba *214, 215*
Elhannani, Aryeh *176, 177, 198*
Engelsberg, Leon 35
Ernst, Max 27
Evron, Hanan *181*
Eytan, D. *196*

Fefferman, Kurt 295, 296, *237*
Feigin, Dov 144, 152, 153, *127, 128, 130*

Italics indicate illustration numbers.

Fima (A. Reutenberg) 41, 42, *80*
Feldman, K. *183*
Feldman, R. *183*
Fichier, Germaine *102*
Fischer, Yona 17
Franck, Joseph 208
Fraenkel, Yitzhak (Frenel) 22, *13*
Fridman, Mira 137
Fromentin 18

Gabo, Nahum 140, *105*
Geddes, Sir Patrick 202
Gernier, Toni 202
Gilad, S. *203*
Giladi, Aharon 23, 30, *7*
Gliksberg, Haim *3*
Goldstein 297
Gonzalezl Julio *107*
Gropius, Walter 211
Gross, Michael 34, 38, *52*
Grossman, Hedwig 292, *250, 252*
Gumbel, David *274–276*
Gumbel, Miriam 297
Gumbel, Mordechai 290, 295, 297, *239*
Gutman, Nahum 18–22, *2*

Haber, Shamai *149*
Hadami, Yehiel 296
Haddad, Avraham 295
Haijm, Kiwe 33
Haikin 210
Halevi, Aharon 19
Halevi, Joseph 37, 38, *74, 75*
Harag-Zunz, Hannah 292, *251*
Harari, Shelli 293, *264, 272*
Harel, Penina 293, *260, 273*
Hareli, Ilana 296
Harrison, 209
Hashimshoni, Avia 199, *205, 206*
Heimann, Shoshana 143, 147, *146, 147*
Hendler, David 22, 23, 42, *36, 37, 38*
Hendrichs, Naomi 297
Herman 211
Hirschenberg 18
Hofmann, Hans 34
Hofstaetter, Osias *24–26*
Holiday, Clifford 210, *160, 161*
Holzmann, 28, 35
Horn 296

Ilan, Eli 143
Idelson, Benjamin 219, *167, 173, 176, 177, 185, 192*

Janco, Marcel 29, 30, 38, *40*
Johnson, Philip 219

Kadish, Miriam 296
Kafka, Franz 36
Kahana, Aharon 31, 40, 293, 294, *93*
Kahn, Louis 217, 219
Kara, Michael 143, 156
Karshi 296
Kaufmann, Richard 207, 208, 210, 225, *158*
Keiner, Julia 290, 296, *262*
Khavkin, D. 227, *203*
Kiffer, Miriam 143
Klarwein 225
Klee, Paul 27, 36, 41
Klein, Alexander 202, 213, 226
Koren, Schlomo 43
Korn, Aryeh 294, *257*
Kosso, Elul 144, 153, *131, 132*
Kossonogi 28
Krakauer, Leopold 25, 210, 212, 213, *10, 11, 163*
Krize, Yehiel 33, 34, *83*

Lalo, Haggit 35, 43, *89*
Lan-Bar, David 47
Larderra, Berto *103*
Lavee, Rafi 43
Lavie, Ruth 296
Le Corbusier, Charles Edouard J. 202, 211, 215, 218, 222, 223, 227
Lehmann, Rudolf 143, 148, 149, 298, *115–119*
Leible, Yaacov 144
Leitersdorf, Fini 298
Levanon, Mordechai 27, 35 *14, 15*
Levenstein, Shulamit 297
Levi, Hannah *51*
Levi-Opel 19
Levine, Avraham 297
Levine, Naomi 297
Levinsky, Elhanan Leib 202
Lilien 17
Lishansky, Batya 143, 144, *109*
Litvinovsky, Pinhas 22, 28, 31, *5*

Loebel, S. V. 298
Loos, Adolf 211, 218
Lorenzeti, Ambrogio 5
Lubin, Arieh 25, 31, *8*
Luchansky, Yaacov 143, 145, *110*

Machs, Yona 25
Mambush, Yitzhak 294
Mansfeld, A. 219, *204*
Marcus, Kaethe-Ephraim 143
Margalit, Aviva 294
Marimel, Marian *99*
Marquet, Albert 27
Marx, Yokheved 293, *268*
Mayo, Nina 40
Mehutan, Hava 143, 146, *150, 151, 152*
Meiselmann-Kluger, Erika 297, *238*
Melnikov, Aharon 19, 142, 143, *108*
Meltzer, S. *180, 202, 207, 208, 215, 220, 221*
Mendelsohn, Erich 210, 211, 212, *164–166*
Merzer, Aryeh 143, *111*
Meshullam, David *88*
Mestiechkin, Shemuel *197,* 211, *224*
Meyer, Yehudit 293, *268*
Meyer, Jean 293, *267*
Meyerovitz, Zvi 30, 33, 34, *39, 70, 71*
Miron, Sima 24
Mokady, Moshe 22, *53, 54, 55*
Moore, Henry *101*
Muller, Otto, 24

Nadler, S. *169, 181*
Naton, 30, 31
Navon, Arieh 23, *49, 50*
Necker 295
Neiman, Yehuda 40
Neufeld, Joseph 212, 213, *174, 175, 178, 179*
Nikel, Lea 42, *45, 46*

Ofek, Avraham 38, *86*
Okashi, Avshalom 30, 35, *84*
Orloff, Hannah 156, *112*

Paldi, Israel 18, 20, 21, 40, *28*
Palombo, David 144, 153, 154, 297, *120*
Pan, Abel 17
Paz, Hayim *247*

Peretz-Arad, Esther *87*
Perret, Auguste 211, 215, 217, 218
Peter, Yohanan 295, *245*
Pevsner, Antoine *104*
Picasso, Pablo Ruiz 10, 32
Pietro, Lorenzo 5
Pins, Yaacob, 25, *65, 66*
Poliakoff, Serge 34
Pozner, S. *181, 222*
Priver, Aharon 143, 145, 156, *113*
Propes 40

Rappaport, Nathan 143
Ratner, Yohanan 208–210, 212, 213, 219, 220, 226, *162, 223*
Rau, Heinz 212, 213, 219, 225, *210, 225*
Rechter, Ze'ev 212, 213, *171, 172, 182, 218*
Reznik, Aryeh 143, *121*
Reznik, D. *225*
Rika 295
Rilke, Rainer Maria 39
Robinson, A. *187*
Rodin, Auguste 137
Rohe, Mies van der 218–219
Rosso, Medardo 137, *100*
Rothchild, Baron Edmond de 203
Roualt, Georges 22, 28
Rousseau, Henry (Douanier) 19
Rubin, Reuven 18–21, 23
Ruppin, Dr. Arthur 208

Samuel Edith 298, *287, 288*
Samuel, Hava *248, 249*
Schacharal-Hilman, Yana 143
Schatz, Bezalel 31, 33, 294, *256*
Schatz, Boris 17, 142, 202, 291
Schatz, Louise 36, *82*
Schatz, Zahara 144, 296, *263, 265*
Schwadron, Madame 296
Schweig, Gedulla 293, 294, *254, 255*
Sebba, Shalom 25, *6*
Senker 211
Shallgi, Y. *187*
Sharon, Aryeh 212, 213, 219, *167, 173, 176, 177, 185, 192*
Shealtiel 296
Shemi, Menahem 18, 21, 35 *41–44*
Shemi, Naomi, *62–63*
Shemi, Yehiel 144, 151, *133–135*
Simon, Yohanan 30, *78*

Soulages, Pierre 39
Soutine, Chaim 22
Stael, Nicholaes de 34, 38, 39
Steinhardt, Yaacov 23, 24, *23*
Steimatzky, Avigdor 23, 30, 32, 33, 42, *16, 17*
Sternschuss, Moshe 143, 149, *122, 123, 125*
Streichman, Yehezkel 30, 32, 33, *67–69*

Tajer, Ziona 18, 20, 21
Tal, Shulamit 294, *243, 258*
Talpir, Gabriel 23
Tamir, Moshe 37, *64*
Tammuz, Benjamin 5, 156, *148*
Tapies, Antonio 41, 43
Ticho, Hannah 25, *12*
Tinguely 140
Tsarfati, Ruth 143, 147–148, 298, *143–145, 282, 283*
Tumarkin, Yigal 43, 144, 154, 155 ,*79, 129*

Uccello, Paolo 11
Uri, Aviva 42, 43, *59, 61*
Urmand, Baruch 297

Villon, Jacques 10
Vitkin, Schlomo 38, 72
Vitkover, Y. *195, 212, 281*

Warshavsky, Neora 296
Wechsler, Jacob 30, 31, *90, 91*
Weinrob, M. 219, *204*
White, Stanford, 202
Winter Fritz, 210
Wolpert, 290
Wright, Frank Lloyd 211, 218, 219

Yanin, Claire 33
Yashar, Y. *196*
Yasky, Abraham *181, 191, 194, 209, 222*

Zarhi, *182, 218*
Zaritzky, Joseph 28–30, 32–33, 35, 43, *29–34*
Ziffer, Moshe 143–145, *124, 126*
Zisselman, Mina 31
Zolotov, Nahum *184, 201*